# Alexandra Mas

# Oh Mother!

ഌ൭ൟ

Publicado por
D'har Services
P.O. Box 290
Yelm, Wa 98597
www.dharservices.com

info@dharservices.com

Cover© Xiomara García

Copyright© 2014 Alexandra Mas

ISBN-13: 978-1-939948-16-8

**Printing in USA**

# Dedication

*To my mother Cruz Burgos, in the Realm of Truth since February12, 2014. Love you forever mami!*

*To Luisa Castillo, my Madre Aguila; for always being there for me.*

*To Rosa Caparros, my Mother in Law; love you much more than you know.*

*To the mother aspect in every human being.*

*To Gaia, our patient and loving Mother Earth.*

# TABLE OF CONTENTS

# FOREWORD

The relationship with our parents does not end with the physical existence of those who embodied that role. Instead, it is better described as an ongoing relationship that we will be recreating throughout our lives with different people, jobs, projects and circumstances. In the relationship with our parents lies the key that will open (or close) the doors that we will encounter in life. As we are usually unaware of this, sometimes we delay the resolution of our conflicts believing that emotional cut-off or distance will help us to overcome them; far from true.

Out of both parents, the mother has the most impacting role, because we were conceived not only in her womb, but amidst her energy. This has consolidated a bond that cannot be destroyed by any form of omission or denial. Because of this, when someone comes into my life I always ask: "How is your relationship with your mother?" Depending on this particular answer, I will be able to understand whatever follows...

To grasp the importance of this important bond is the greatest challenge of humanity because we're not born with instructions on how to achieve a successful one. Just as we hear people saying, "Nobody teaches us how to be parents," we could also complain that nobody taught us how to be sons or daughters. However, both arguments will lose strength by the time you are done learning, reflecting and finding inspiration in these pages.

A great challenge such as this calls for a great psychotherapist.

Alexandra Mas is the right person to guide us through that process. We do not always come across a great psychotherapist who has also accomplished a high level of personal human development, and who is capable of providing us with a vision about a life's situation that is real, possible and profound. I can assure you that this is not just "another book", nor Alexandra Mas is not just "another author". In the following pages, you will be able to relate to each of the clients' stories as if they were your own, and you will receive Alexandra's message as if she was speaking to you face-to-face; with compassion, certainty and wisdom. Just as a mother willing to reconnect us with the greatest love we can experience in our human journey.

Julio Bevione
New York, August 2013

# PREFACE

The premise of this book is that a mother can never harm her child.

It's true that some mothers elicit a soulful: "Oh Mother!" But, as free decision makers, my invitation is for us to accept the responsibility for the mother we have, because at some level we have chosen her or attracted her.

Our mother is our first mirror and the best teacher to incorporate that core lesson that we haven't managed to learn.

Since I published the original version of this book (*Historias que son... ¡De Madre!*) in 2013, I've been asked: "Why are women to blame"? My explanation is that a mother is never guilty, but always a protagonist. So mothers: Since we have the huge responsibility to breed and nurture life, let's exert maternity with consciousness because our actions and/or inactions will imbue each life with either happiness, or unhappiness.

Regardless of whether you are a mother or not, you have been born to one... so then, read without judgment, but with reverence!

Alexandra Mas
Boston, March 2014

Alexandra Mas

# *Acknowledgements*

*To my husband Oscar Mas, for your daily encouragement and constant challenge.*

*To the Yin-Yang of my life, Mario and Pablo Garcia, my sons and Aynet Bustillo, my daughter-in-law (the daughter I never had). Thanks for your collaboration in the translation of this book.*

*To the brave women who opened their hearts to share their "Oh Mother!" stories. Thanks to you, many people will have the opportunity to understand their own dynamics, and be able to help themselves.*

*To you, the reader of this book, my gratitude and a request: send your blessings to the protagonists of these stories. Although their names have been changed to protect their identities, they will receive them; The Accounting System of the Universe is Perfect.*

*The stories in this book are presented from the perspective of the consultants, not of the author.*

*As such, the narration may look disorganized and/or blurry. However, these are essential features that help us to understand the psychological moment in which these clients found themselves at the time they seek help to change and grow.*

**I**

# "My reflection on the mirror"
*The story of Ximena, 37 years old*

I suffer from insomnia and chronic fatigue. I haven't slept in 23 years; since I was 14 years old.

My dad was an alcoholic, neurotic and abuser. He used to come home between 11:00 PM and 1:00 AM. For me, it was like a demon had arrived. He would start beating my mother up as soon as he had come through the door. A couple of times he almost killed her! I couldn't do anything to help her; I was scared of him.

I remember one day when we got in the car, and he immediately grabbed my mother by the hair; he smashed her face into the windshield. She was pregnant with my youngest sister, who's a marked woman to this day. My oldest sister was spared because since my grandmother felt alone, she went to live with my grandparents. She –my oldest sister– rejected me since I was born, and did not speak to me.

We used to get kicked out of every house we lived in; we lost every one of them! My grandfather, bless his heart, sheltered us every time. One day however, he decided to kick my father out of his house. If it wasn't for that, my mother wouldn't have left him! Those were difficult times, because my mother had never worked or studied before. My oldest sister took on the role as the family provider. She's ill mannered, but well, I must concede that she never took time off, and always shared her money with the family.

My younger sister –born immediately after me– is happily married to another completely dysfunctional man, whom never studied anything. His formal degrees are: ex-alcoholic and ex-addict. We don't know how come she's so happy in her co-dependency with her husband. She has no money, no clothes... she has nothing! Yet, she's very happy! Their children are both mistakes. I don't know why, but everyone in the family – including me – treats her very bad and we hate her as much as we hate her husband. We support them, regardless of how burdensome they are. She is my favorite sister, but she doesn't speak; she doesn't express herself. I feel as if I pushed my mother to love her. I told her: "Don't love me if you don't want to, love my sister because she is there with you"... but she never did. I feel sympathy and pity for my sister. I try to help her but her ego doesn't allow her to receive. One day I told her: "I'm sorry that you are with that person. I can feel your low self-esteem. I'm sorry that you don't want to grow. It makes me angry to see that you reject my attentions. I'm hurt to see that I'm not important to you!"

pg. 16

My brother, the only boy in the family, is the love of all. He has two degrees; he is an artist. In the past, he was the most sick among us, neurotic and aggressive. Well, he's still super-neurotic, but he loves us all. My sisters deal with him in fear, because they never know when they will trigger him.

Me, I'm the quality control for this family.

I grew up in the midst of religion, with a great deal of conflict with the idea of sin. I had pre-marital sex but I didn't enjoy it. After getting married, I did have some purely sexual relationships, and they were wonderful. My husband is low in testosterone and he is an incompetent lover. I have come to the conclusion that I didn't complete the sexual stage of my life; I didn't live it. When we got married, he didn't know anything about it. At the moment he was not a religious man, but he became one afterwards. My marriage can be summarized in 3 months of super wow, and then ten years waiting...

I had spent twenty years living outside of my country, and I went on two months of vacation. I was very excited... I think I had idealized all my family members. My oldest sister didn't speak to me on the phone, or came to meet her nephew. She was the same unloving person and I hated her guts. One day I told her: "I recognize the love and care that you've had towards our mother, but I detest that you are so ungrateful. Now, she is married to an abusive man.

Mom would take advantage of any given opportunity to flee out the back door, and when she stayed, she seemed absent... Before returning I confronted her: "I can understand that you don't love me, but I can't understand that you don't love my son, why don't you love him?"

"Your son is a spoiled brat!" she said.

"Why? Because the kid can actually open his mouth and let you know what you need to hear or because he put you in place by setting limits and is able to say 'no'? I replied. Then I thought to myself, "This old bitch doesn't love me!" So I told her, "Do you know what, mother? I did my part and you failed to do yours. It seems as if I'm the only one who accepts her own mistakes." She quickly retorted, as if it wasn't a big deal: "You're right." She said; she turned around, and left.

That day I divorced her. Now I understand why she never called me during all those years! I should've got the message a few years before, when I asked her once: "Do I buy you a plane ticket so you can come visit?" Her response was: "Why don't you send me a ticket to go to Las Vegas? I would love to go there!" That day I cried. I went to a psychologist who told me: "She's playing the victim's role, and you are the bad one because in your attempt to defend her, you are fighting with everyone." I finally got the memo...

That night, I wrote a lengthy letter to my mother and another to my father.

*Mom,*

*You married a neurotic and egocentric man. It hurts me that you never protected me, or stood up for* me. I'm sorry that you chose that man as my father. I'll never understand why you could never leave him, or why you continued to have kids with him. However, I admire that you didn't get caught up, trapped in the past, like me... Simply and plainly, you moved on with your life as if nothing had happened, and now, you even have some booze and get drunk!

You gave me what you could; always found a way to give me a present on my birthdays, despite us not having much. I thought that was very nice of you, but it makes me mad that you didn't leave my father any sooner!

\*\*\*\*\*

Dad,

My dear alcoholic and aggressive one, I despise you. I'm revolted by your ego. I don't understand how you manage to not ask for forgiveness. I always dreamed that you came back to tell us how much you had been mistaken and how sorry you were for the shitty life you gave us. I love that you are intelligent and cultured, but I hate it when I hear you speaking on a podium. I'm fascinated by the finesse with which you treat those who are not your family.

Thank you; you showed me another world when we traveled together. I delight in knowing that you haven't lost your spark, but it hurts to know that you didn't shine. I'm sorry that you couldn't stop being an alcoholic. I always thought I would be able to help you, but I couldn't... I can forgive you for being lazy and irresponsible...but I can't forgive your alcoholism!

\*\*\*\*\*

Since I felt the words came straight from my soul, I decided to go see him before my return. It turned out that he was admitted to a rehab center for the poor. It was a horrible, seedy place. I found that he, who is just sixty years old, has been peeing and shitting on his pants for the past three years... I've suffered greatly since I saw him, because I can't help him.

I have felt disabled and out of focus since that trip. I suffer from attachments. Everything that I've studied is going to waste because of the language barrier... is killing me!

I'm tired of my husband; I don't like him anymore. I've been longing to get a divorce for years on end. I panic to think that I will not achieve happiness, because I have never been happy.

Now I constantly dream of a boyfriend that I once had, very handsome and very violent; I was so in love with him!

I've become my mother... she's my reflection on the mirror!

## Ximena's Case Analysis

Ximena is an emotional and anxious person. The task ahead of her is to learn to be sensitive, without being so emotional.

The daughter of an alcoholic father and a co-dependent mother, she witnessed many things that no one should see; for certain, a small child is not mature enough to understand such things, or make any sense of them.

Like any other good girl, she loves both her parents, which is why she fears for her mother's life whenever her father is beating her up; but she also fears for her father, if indeed he were to kill her mother. What consequences would he have to face as a result of his deeds? What would that mean for the family and more in specific, to her? These are some of the unanswered questions that she has had to grow up with, as the daughter of an abusive parent, alcoholic or not. In addition to that, there is the nonsense of why her father does not love her mother, or why she does not love herself enough to leave him. Instead she stays with him, putting the lives of her children in danger, when parents are supposed to take care of, and protect their children.

Her first male and female role models, as well as the example of what a couple is supposed to be, are terrifying. As such, and deep inside of her, she does everything she can to avoid becoming a full grown woman. This in turn, would prevent her from "turning into her mother," and would protect her from attracting a man like her father.

This is the reason why Ximena does not have a happy relationship. She did not marry for love; she chose a man based on what she did not want. By marrying someone different from her father, she reassures herself that she is different from her mother. This is why she feels horrified when she realizes that she has fallen into the same pattern of behavior. Thus, she allows the abuse from her husband; not and active, enacted abuse, but an abuse by omission, a passive one. The man is expected to provide sex and livelihood, biologically speaking. Her father seemed to have provided sex, but no livelihood. Ximena's husband does not provide her with sex, but he does provide certain monetary stability that allows her to be the "good person" that helps her family of origin.

Ximena loves her family of origin, yet her insecure attachment leads to her ambivalent behavior. It is the same love-hate relationship between her parents which molds and defines her relationship with the members of her family. She projects onto her siblings all the aspects of her that she denies. What she needs to see in her siblings –especially in her "favorite" sister– is the reflection of her own marital unhappiness. When she appoints herself as the "quality control" for her family, she blinds herself from her own *unfinished business*. So, she has yet to break the pattern of abuse and co-dependency.

Her fear of lack is kept in place by sustaining a relationship without love; a reflection of her own lack of self-love. What looks like dishonesty and unfaithfulness at a first glance, is nothing more than an escape mechanism that does not allow her to come to a resolution. She does not get a divorce, amongst other reasons, so she can differentiate herself from her parent's behavior. She has decided to turn the father of her son into her own personal savior, because her ego does not allow her to ask for help. When she finally reaches for help, she does not get it, and as a result, she feels even more disabled and her symptoms only get worse; consequently, she remains in her *comfort zone.*

Since Ximena has been an *emotional orphan* and her parents are still alive, she yearns for them to eventually behave as she would have liked them to, as parents should; hence, she continues to behave like a child. This is typical behavior of adult children of alcoholics (specially the aggressive type), in the *irrational belief* that they cannot allow themselves to grow up until that role model redeems itself in front of them, by accepting his mistakes and asking for forgiveness... which rarely happen. Ximena then goes into the realm of her imagination, and re-creates the image of both her parents in order to (emotionally) survive.

The image of her "father" turns into the *archetype* of the ideal man for Ximena. This imaginary concept of an ideal man is not going to materialize and rescue her to live happily ever after.

She has a greater challenge with her mother, and that is that it appears as if she –the mother– managed to overcome her years of abuse and co-dependency without the need for excuses or asking for forgiveness. Ximena's perplexity is why she failed do it before, when she was clearly capable of doing so. As a result, instead of her father being the villain of the movie, and her mother being the victim, it turns out that now the mother is the villain that made her and her siblings undergo many years of suffering fear and shame… It is her lack of acceptance of her mother which leads her one day to recognize that the ideal image of a mother that she has recreated is none other than herself. She is incapable of rescuing her mother from within herself, so she ends up mired in despair.

The *programming conflict* that affects her sleeping pattern is the fact that Ximena's father used to abuse her mother during "sleep time," which is why the nighttime, becomes dangerous. The appropriate course of action is, apparently, to remain awake and vigilant… It is assumed that the threat was supposed to have been eliminated at some point in time but this never happened, so, the sustained state of alertness turned into chronic fatigue.

Although Ximena attributes her underachievement to w2hat she calls the language barrier, what in fact paralyzes her constant state of worry and self-pity. Like the prototypic anxious person, she has blocked her capacity to live in the present moment; she continuously recreates her past by talking about it, and wastes her time looking for signs that will reassure her of her need to worry… and of course, she finds them. She has the obsession that something bad is going to happen.

On the other hand, the inability to learn any subject points to a "know-it-all" attitude. When one knows it all… what is there to learn?

This is a great time for Ximena because she has started to make sense of past opportunities for growth that she has missed, and she is accepting of her material attachments; she's in the right path for healing.

*"I have learned that regardless of your relationship with your parents, you will miss then when they are gone."*

Maya Angelou

## *Ximena's Action Protocol:*

1. *Recognize that your worrisome, and fearful thoughts, block and consume your energy.*
2. *Confront the voices of your past with authority. Say: "Enough is enough! This is it! Today I reclaim my present!"*
3. *Begin to appreciate everything that you have in your life at this moment.*
4. *Spend some time each day experiencing with all your senses anything and everything that seems to be pleasant at any given moment.*
5. *Give yourself the right to have needs. Explain them, ask for help to the appropriate person and create a network of support with the understanding that just because you ask for something, it does not mean that you are going to get it.*
6. *Become aware that you do not need to prove anything. Just give yourself permission to be*

*yourself, with your* strengths and weaknesses, *like anybody else.*

7. *Make a list of the things you would like to do; establish at least one short-term goal, a medium-term goal, and a long-term goal.*

8. *Develop a plan to carry them out, and perform a specific action each day to achieve those goals.*

9. *Visualize at every opportunity you have, even while multitasking. Instead of worrying, use your fertile imagination and your energy load in order to attract only what you want.*

10. *From time to time, and deliberately, let yourself go in the face of the unknown... trust that your intuition will guide you, give it a chance!*

# II

# It killed me!

*The story of Andrea, 56 years old*

I dread to have cancer. I went to the doctor for my annual mammogram and I have a cyst in the left breast. I'm vegetarian and naturist, so I allowed conventional practitioners to perform a thermogram and a sonogram, but not a biopsy. I'm here to explore other possibilities.

I had an abortion at age 33. I was single and afraid. It was a casual partner. I would have wanted the baby, but the man was a womanizer... a gorgeous one! Ever since I can remember, my mother use to tell me what was a good catch, and he definitely wasn't. When he learned of the abortion, he rebuked me: "Why didn't you ask me? I may have wanted the little one!" But I did it and I felt good about it. Little did I know that was my only chance in to be a mom! It wasn't the right moment, I still lived with my parents and I wasn't free. My mother micromanaged my every move; I was fully controlled. Not because she loved me so much, but because she was interested in the money I brought home. My mother always said that you are what you own. She oversaw everybody's money and never lifted a finger!

In my fear of not being able to sustain myself financially on my own, I stuck with that unfair situation until I got married at age 35. I was an old fart! One fine day I told myself: "It's time to leave home and get married". The first person I met I qualified as "the right person." I didn't really analyze the situation. His mother didn't like me, but that played in my favor, for we immediately came to live in this country. I didn't come following his pants, but I needed a change. Escape from my bossy mother, that house and my country. By then, I was ready to have a baby, and he agreed. We wanted, but we couldn't... I recently looked at my natal chart, and my house of children is empty...

At first my husband was very nice; he protected me and we used to enjoy everything. But now... oh my! His character is so negative! He wakes up with a shitty face. He is a very good companion; a good person, but there were always arguments. One time he left for a month; when he came back, and in the midst of my cold and calculating heart, I asked him how we were going to manage our finances. He was suddenly quiet and I spit to his face: "You live in a cloud of fart." I now see that he was never organized, and he got himself someone OCD lady boss capable of breaking his balls. I'm always organized with money; he is very sloppy.

One time I was so fed up that I wanted out. "How can I still be married to you?" I screamed. "We are like oil and water!" Only when he faces adversity, does he behave as he should. Once he was very ill. He went with me to do yoga, A Course in Miracles and Kabbalah classes, Reiki sessions... you name it! As soon as he began to recover, he stopped coming. Now he should be watching his diet, he doesn't; he's not supposed to drink alcohol and he does... I'm not a control freak, but I'm certainly not his mother. "It's your life! Take care of yourself!" I say to him. But my words fall on deaf hears. When we are angry I call him 'roommate.' He doesn't even care. His priorities are: soccer, everything else, and then... me.

There are things I would not put up with anymore... We are parallel to one another; there's no converging point! In fact, there isn't even a sexual relationship... as such. It hurts with, or without lubrication; the sensation is so horrendous that he can't even penetrate me. He loves me and acts accordingly. From time to time he asks: "Is this even normal?" I tell him that sometimes there's a lack of lubrication during menopause. So, when that needs to happen, we do other things; without penetration.

The issue is that I'm afraid. Afraid to start a new relationship, afraid to be alone, afraid to fail, and even more afraid to return back home... To go back implies going back to my mother and what people will say about it. I think I would be mortified. To find myself with all the family that stood in time, who are now just as they were when I left, or maybe worse. The very thought of it makes me want to kill myself because reality is... I escaped!

Dad was the love of my life... he was a good father. Always supported me and gave me strength. When he passed away I was here as an illegal alien; I couldn't see him in his final moment. He was already sick when I left, but I braved it out. Abandonment is not forgiven in Italian families. I'm sure they said: "She went away with her macho and left her ill father behind" Maybe even I thought so too... He said goodbye to me on the same day I told him I was leaving; I remember his sad face. I didn't feel guilty right that moment, for I knew I was running away for my sanity.

He was a quiet man, my father...my mother talks too much! "I'm perfect," she always says. "I don't hurt anyone" hum! I love her because she is my mother... I guess...I don't know! I can't change her; I wanted to, I tried to but... mom's a handful!

Sometimes it takes me a month to gather the courage to call her, because I fight with her even over the phone. She says: "Why don't you call often? I am still alive!" When I talk to her I get hot flashes... She complains about her sister, says she is no good, then about her brother who according to her is even worse... She doesn't go visit them because she says that they're disgusting; her own blood! She even bad mouths her friends behind their backs! When she talks like that I keep my mouth shut. "Are you there, my daughter?" she asks. "Yes, mother," I answer, as if with my acknowledgement I grant her my permission to criticize humanity... She gives to you, and then she takes from you. She sucks up your energy... she drains you! My dad was the opposite; he would be there for you, would solve things easily... My mom, if she had the chance, she'd hurt you!

You had to listen to the language my mother used with us as children, and with my father... Also, she used to hit us a lot; it was like some sort of imperative need of hers! You couldn't speak; she would slap you or throw something at you. She would throw shoes, brushes, medicine bottles... whatever! My mother was more sensitive perhaps towards a dog... She was always quick to point out our errors and flaws... Oh Mother! I was always very hairy, so she used to call me "hairy cockroach"... it hurt! That's how one grows up collecting emotional garbage.

I was scarred by many things… taking my baby away… not having my mother by my side whenever I needed her… particularly during that process. She still doesn't know to this day.

At times I see myself and think that I'm the reflection of my mother; I am my mother! One day I slapped my husband in the face for lying to me… A typical reaction of hers! I was horrified; so inappropriate and disrespectful of me. My mother didn't love my father. She only married him because my grandmother told her: "He is a good catch; marry him" and that was it. Whenever I saw that he wasn't feeling well, I'd tell him: "Dad, leave my mother" or "If I was you, I would've left." He never responded, until the day of our farewell… He looked at me in the eye and said: "Enough of that! Don't you see I love your mother?" It killed me!

## Andrea's Case Analysis

To fear something is a sure way to attract it; it is the reason why Andrea finally sought help. She arrives with a *diagnosis conflict*, and does not know how to get out of the wheel of fear and somatization. Her will to not cut, poison, or burn her body (through surgery, chemotherapy or radiation), is key to unlocking her ability to express the resentment she holds within, from all the mother/daughter conflict that she has been holding back. At first, she thinks that her issues relate to her husband –and she is not that mistaken– but she quickly realizes that what is really bothering her is her *childhood wound of injustice*, due to the relationship with her mother. She feels that she needs her mother, the archetypal mother that nurtures in all aspects, but instead she gets a mother that devalues her.

Andrea lives searching for her father in every man she encounters, but since in order to have your father you have to be like your mother, she makes sure that she finds someone different for her. First of all, in the relationship she had with the "gorgeous womanizer", but that somehow did not fit the mold her mother (as well as her grandmother) had labeled as a "good catch". It seems as if she did not consult with anybody, for she made the decision to have an abortion all by herself, without letting the father of the child know about it. She did consult about one thing, though, and that was the *program* she had *introjected* from her mother and grandmother, with regards to what a "good catch" is, or not. Reality is that she did not have the freedom to make up her own mind, so what she ultimately aborted was her *life project*. This is the reason why she refused to go through with her creation; in this case, the product of that relationship. To be able to live with her consciousness, she justified and rationalized her decision, but she became infertile because she felt too guilty. Although she lived that guilt in denial, she felt she had to punish herself. She again punishes herself unconsciously for the guilt of not being present at her father's death bed. She refuses to grieve her loss so her feelings turn into *pathological grief.*

It is typical for women to develop problems with their genital organs, or sexual intercourse related issues after an abortion. It happens as a form of self-punishment, because the woman cannot find another way to cope with the strong sense of guilt and shame for having interrupted a human life. It is an unconscious mechanism, of course, but it is real; guilt always begets punishment. In the particular case of Andrea, it manifests in the form of sexual frustration. The vaginal dryness that she experiences is a rejection to the act of penetration, which she does not equate to pleasure, but to the impossibility of procreation.

Andrea's breast cyst is the somatization of her perception of her mother's attack on her dignity, and there is more. It also evidences her sense of separation from her father and now from her husband as well as a feeling of abandonment from her mother and ultimately from her own self.

Andrea will have to gain awareness of her *introjection* of the concepts "good catch" and "the right one", because they are not hers. What her mother told her, which is what her grandmother told her mother, is a great example of *transgenerational transmission*. To become aware of this will heal her female ancestors, and uproot the curse for the following generations. Although she did not have children of her own, she does have blood ties, and healing operates by *quantum entanglement*. After all, she was the chosen one –by herself – of the clan to transmute that discordant energy, and by that, liberate her family tree from its noxious effects.

*"The journey begins with the discovery, not merely with the information."*

Thomas Keating

## Andrea's Action Protocol:

1. In a very relaxed state imagine that you gave life to the soul whose life you took. Feel the pregnancy, visualize yourself in labor, give the kid a name and be a mother throughout the stages of life. This will bring closure to all involved and will also give you the opportunity to live the experience that you denied yourself. The brain does not distinguish between reality and imagination.
2. Identify and face the *introjections* that you internalized from your mother that have created programmed decisions such as, but not limited to the "good catch," the "right person," "you are what you own," etc. Imagine that you get them all in a suitcase, and tell her firmly in your mind: "Mother, this is not mine. I give it back to you!"
3. Heal the perplexity that you felt because your father never left your mother and stop being controlling; do not get involved in other people's affairs.

4. Forgive your mother, and reconciliate your feminine and masculine *aspect*s. Only then, will there be an available place for your partner in your life.
5. Accept that your father cannot take the place of your partner. In the *clan*'s hierarchy your father precedes you and your partner stands by your side.
6. Recognize that at some point you "used" your husband in order to advance your agenda and honor him because he has been there for you throughout your journey.
7. Admit that you chose your husband –and continue to do so– based on love, and re-negotiate in good faith the terms of your relationship. Allow yourself to enjoy pleasure and happiness
8. Treasure your father's example of commitment and dedication –not sacrifice– in the name of love, as well as, his ability to take complete responsibility for the circumstances of his life.
9. Share your secrets with your mother, and encourage her to tell you hers; in this way, you will both heal. When you abandon the "victim" role, slowly but surely she will abandon hers, because it will no longer be needed in your "drama."
10. Since you have become a very structured person, recognize that you just have imprisoned yourself with those walls. Bring some down so you can flow more easily with life.

# III

## "It devastates me"

*The story of Yves, 45 years old*

I have a great life and a cool son, but I haven't had a partner in 11 years. I am the problem; I know. I make the same mistake, over and over. I'm OCD, and I get attached. I become a brat all of a sudden; impulsive, and so, history always repeats. I look for a partner because one cannot be happy without one. It is a law of life that everything has to be in pairs. But it's not in my hands! In fact, I have been haunted by a repetitive dream for some time now. In the dream, I'm completely in love with a guy, but he abandons me and leaves me for another woman! I never see his face, but it is always the same dream...

I got married when I was 20 years old, and got divorced at 24. He loved me and I loved him, but he slept with my best friend. Reality is that at some point I wanted to leave him, so it hurt me more because of my friend, than because of him.

Then, I had another relationship, with the man who would be the father of my son, but it ended right after. We have only seen him three times in 15 years…

My hands have been shaking for a month now. My mother's shake too, for two years now. It seems to be a congenital condition that I hope I have not inherited. I don't sleep. Only five hours: from 10:00 PM to 3:00 AM. I suffer from major depression. I've been taking some experimental medication for the last four months, as a part of a clinical trial.

When my parents were still married, my mother's world revolved around my sister; she didn't care to make it obvious! In order to compensate, my father made his world revolve around me. I was daddy's queen, his princess. Everything changed after the divorce; I was left alone and I was only nine years old… From time to time he would show up to ask my mother to come back, or he'd come looking for us with a different woman every time... That really affected me! He died of a cerebral stroke at the age of seventy one.

It doesn't hurt me much to be abandoned by a man as much as it hurt me to see him later with another woman… It hurts me terribly! The same hurt that I felt every time I saw my father with another woman… It torned me apart!

I have done two regressions in my life; one with the Scientologists, and another one with Brian Weiss. Through that one I learned that when I was born, my father really wanted a boy… I was his disappointment! The first regression sessions lasted approximately six months. They took me back, further back and way back. Little by little they took me back in time. Scientologists want you to remember everything that has ever happened in your total existence as a soul. They say that knowledge is like a chain: the links cannot have gaps. I saw myself as a fetus; one eye bigger than the other. I heard my mother talking to some lady who appeared to be my godmother... I can still hear her voice in my head: "I'm pregnant and my husband had a baby girl with another woman." All of the sudden I felt what she felt: she didn't want to have me! That was my first depression. Not only wasn't I wanted as a girl... I wasn't wanted at all!

I only have one older sister. I would have had a brother, but he was born dead. As young girls, my sister was hyperkinetic; now it's me. I was very pretty and everybody noticed me. They would say: "the little one this, the little one that." Then, my sister would attack me. And I mean it; she would attack me a lot! I was always bruised or scratched. They used to call my mother from school, but she never did anything about it. So, the abuse went on; I was severely abused by my sister during childhood!

When my mother re-married, my father totally disappeared from our lives; that's it, vanished, as if we didn't exist. For some reason, my mom wanted to prove to the man that she had a good family. It was the best time of my life! The four of us did things together like any normal family would. To me, he is my father, although she says that he doesn't love me. He is all adoration with my son, unlike my dad who never even met him...

At some point, I don't know what my mother said to the guy, that for a while he changed his behavior toward me. When I was about 14 years old, I had it, and I told her: "Since I don't belong to this family, then I belong in the streets!" I left my family, for they were very damaging to me. I ended up raising myself, looking for what I was missing in my friends' families... I grew up with a huge sense of loneliness. Finally I moved here and I married the father of my son; another piece of garbage who abandoned me like my dad did.

My mother continued to reject me throughout my life. It was only about three years ago that things changed; I also learned to manipulate! Now, when she calls me I answer the phone by saying: "Hello, this is your favorite daughter speaking," instead of fanning the flame. I also became a Christian for twelve years, and God performed a miracle for me, for our relationship. I stopped being a Christian because God didn't perform very miracle that I wanted, and that was to have a husband. I still believe in God, but not in preachers... not anymore. I used to believe in mine blindly, and everything that he asked, I did with faith. He made me do a whole myriad of things... One was a treasure map to attract my soul mate... In the end, I became angry with him and never went back to church. It was a shame because I prayed for a lot of people...

I just went back to my country after a gazillion years of living abroad... It looked like Hiroshima after the atomic bomb! Regardless of what happens there, the encounter with my sister was... my God... we have nothing in common! She has no personality; I got it all! She is so insecure that I would never have her as a friend. She is selfish and a backstabber. I saw her so insignificant! Like nothing... Like a car with no air conditioning or automatic windows...

My father had his stroke while I was there, and my sister practically kidnapped me to force me to go visit. I was so pissed, that I cursed in the car, all the way to the hospital. There I met dad's children; they hugged me and said: "Thank you for coming." "Don't thank me! I replied "I'm here against my will!"

I was told that my father couldn't recognize anyone, as if I cared about it; to me, the man was nobody... I didn't feel a thing. When he saw me, the man became desperate; "Oh, so now you want to talk!" I scream at him. I was so angry that I didn't go to him in fear that I may slap him in the face. From afar I said: "If someone doesn't love you, why would you want that person close to you?" All of the sudden I realized that he was just like my son's father, so there and then I dumped both scumbags out of my heart...

I closed the cycle with that country and with those people...

If I don't think about me not having a life partner, I am fine. My son is "my husband"; he already assumed the role. The thing is that since he doesn't have a girlfriend either, he says that he inherited from me the gene with the "inability to have a life partner" trait... we laugh, but it's not funny...

## Yves' Case Analysis

Yves wishes to understand why is it that while she has a good life, she cannot keep a relationship. This is her explicit perplexity, but there is an implicit one: her inability to enjoy what she has by the mere fact that she does not have a life partner...

It would be obvious to think that it is because she was raised without a father, but there is more to it.

As a female, Yves was not desired by her father, and she was unconsciously rejected by the mother who, while pregnant with her, learned that her husband had had another baby girl out of wedlock. This could be the reason why her mother never really gets to love her, because Yves reminds her that her husband's lover and her baby girl came first; a painful episode of her life...

In order for a child of divorced parents to grow up without the traumas related to the separation of the family, the child needs to feel the love and attention of both parents, and know that they appreciate and respect each other as the mother and father of their child. The child also needs a place; a symbolic place, and a real place. Every member of a family has a place in the *clan*. Transgenerational therapy provides the interesting concept of *invisibility.* The invisible members of a clan are those whose voice is not heard, and whatever they do, nobody takes into consideration. Unless they get attention through negative behavior, but then of course, they become the black sheep, thus the *scapegoat* of the family. From a psychoanalyst's perspective, one could say that Yves's place is the *no-place*, precisely because she was not desired and nobody was truly expecting her; her father was in another relationship, and her mother was in the place of a victim…

Yves unconsciously repeats the pattern of the absent man. She longs for a significant other and has no problem attracting men; however there is no way she can keep any. This is the reason she makes sure that she only has one male child, who is the substitute for the alpha male that has never remained in her life. She even chooses an absent father for her son. To make matters worse, her belief that she needs to have a man in her life leads her to fill that void with her son, and she fools herself thinking that he goes along and does it willingly… Thus, she underestimates her son's complaints due to her own longing to sustain a relationship.

What Yves resents the most about her father is not that he abandoned her, but the fact that he left her alone with her mother (and sister, who is the *symbolic-double* of the mother). If her brother had lived, she would have had an ally in him, but he also left her alone. Having been named as a boy (the feminine version of her name is Yvette), even though it is a foreign name, has branded her with a male identity. If we apply Dr. Salomon Sellam's theory of the "yaciente", one could say that she carries the load of a masculine energy that could be that of her deceased brother. She could also be hiding a suppressed desire to be a male, in the belief that if she had been a boy, her father would not have abandoned her. In this sense, it is very obvious that she has a need to differentiate herself from the women in her life —mother and sister— because she never felt loved by them; on the contrary, she felt injured. Either way, it is clear that the place of a man in Yves's life is already been fulfilled...by herself!

The condition with her hands also points to the father. The father acts as the guideline for her choice of a couple, and he also establishes the parameters by which Yves will know whether a man deserves her or not. With her father's disappearance, Yves has lost all those patterns of reference... In addition, etymologically speaking, the hand represents manipulation. According to the Bioneuroemotion, resentment says: "I am under the impression that I am being manipulated." But her hands also tremble because of the additional pressure to get away from her mother, whose hands also tremble. The fact that she is experiencing such symptoms might be a call from her subconscious to remember that she chose herself to be the one to heal her family tree. In any case, her desire to control the circumstances of her life is such that she develops a tremble, which might be an early sign of Parkinson's disease.

Her insomnia is related to the grief for a father who was dead to her when she needed him the most, well before he actually died. Depression is a means to relief some of the pressure derived from the beliefs created as a result of a truncated childhood, and her frustration as a woman that can't find a suitable couple. She would like to despise men but she cannot because it is her only son who provides her with a measure of love, support and understanding that she is always searched for. Her inability to accept this, leads her to undervalue her son; and in her continuous clinging to dissatisfaction, she keeps her son tied up...

It is also interesting to observe the anger she feels toward the priest; another man in her life that abandoned her, though symbolically, because she feels the disappointment. One cannot forget to mention the ultimate disappointment, that of the God Father archetype, who denied her of the miracle that she asked for, and only brought her mother closer...She, seeks "revenge" by means of not praying "for a lot of people." It would be interesting to hear the words of her prayers, to see just how far she was meddling in other people's affairs. She pretended to help them, without even having the ability to help herself...

*"You are a desired being: you were born because the Universe wanted it."*

Alejandro Jodorowsky

## Yves' Action Protocol:

1. *Go in search of your inner child, give her everything she still wishes for, and help her to grow up to your present age. Otherwise, she will continue to give you trouble and get in the way of all your relationships.*
2. *Understand that it was your wounded child who decided to divide the world between those who manipulate, and those that are manipulated. Be proactive and choose a paradigm that befits who you wish to be today.*
3. *Stop generalizing, both "men" and "women," according to what you learned from the first role models in your life. If you hold true that all men abandon and/or are trash, and that all women are betrayers, incapable of loving, then, who are you? And, what will it be of your son? If you wish to leave a good legacy, then turn yourself into an honest person,*

capable of loving. When this becomes the new you, you will attract into your life according to this, and as such, you will attract the partner that you desire and will have the family that you have always wanted.

4. Recognize that even though your parents did not love you as you thought they should have, they loved you in the best way they knew and could.

5. Stop searching for a guru. There is no searching; only being. That can only be achieved by making new decisions based on what you want to create.

# IV

## "Stop the World; I want to get off!"
### *The story of Sofia, 43 years old*

I am super depressed in the midst of this change. What I mostly feel is fear and anger. I am very insecure, and I need to learn how to manage my anger!

I have always suffered from depression, and my tendency has been to close myself off. My father is manic depressive and my mother has a borderline personality disorder. Mom could equally wake me up with kisses, or yelling. She says that she didn't breastfeed me because "that wasn't the norm" during those times. Always very particular with regards to physical contact; if I was sick, she would cuddle with me, otherwise, she wouldn't even pay attention to me!

My mom told me once, in a not so healthy manner, that she discovered my dad had another child when she was pregnant with me: "Those are accidents that happen in life," she said. Then, she sentenced: "You can't trust anyone."

It was somewhat of a paradox: "I love you very much," used to say my mother, but she pushed me around. I used to do everything thinking, "My God, I hope she doesn't get mad!" It didn't happen every day, but she'd get mad way too often. She was always aggressive in her way of speaking; a time came when I just got used to her yelling and throwing things at me. However, to this day I react very badly when I am afraid… It was craziness keeping a secret in the midst of such madness!

One day my mom got really pissed; I don't know what I did. My favorite toy was a cash machine that she had given to me as a present. She threw it on the floor and smashed it. It blew me away to see that behavior, breaking something. After that, she slammed the door behind herself, pretended like she was leaving, and then she hid herself.

At first I thought, "Thank goodness she left!" But afterwards, it felt horrible to think that she had abandoned me…A few days later, as if nothing had happened, she bought me another cash machine. Years later I thought: "She's quite the son a bitch!" The woman was really perverted.

When I was seven years old, I had a teacher who made me the center of attention in front of the whole class. I thought to myself: "I am so stupid." I was a good girl and the teacher noticed that about me. Before that episode I used to feel normal, like the rest of my class. After that, I always felt so stupid. I would fake pains in order to skip school...I almost flunked that school year!

My older brother was intelligent and diligent with the studies. He's been married for years...His relationship saved him! He came to this country years later...I was horrified at the idea that he had left me alone with my parents! At fifteen years old I was still a little girl, and I was not prepared to confront that reality...

I was always in anguish. My life consisted of a lot of crying and passiveness...with that thing of not being loved...

Sometime later I was diagnosed with anemia. They took me to the doctor because I was always tired; always in the clouds! From that moment on, the psychoanalysts' parade began...I was always in therapy!

Once I was of age, I felt a killer pain whenever my mother spoke to me with anger; pure psychic agony. One day I had the following thought: "I will take no more of this shit." I didn't express it verbally, but I struck my fist hard on the table; I had a bruise on my hand for three days...But my mother didn't say a word! That day, I felt the anger in the mouth of my stomach, and it was visceral...primitive...

When I came to this country I learned, for the first time in my life, that I could live without crying. I was surprised! However, there still remained a core level of melancholy that was already mine...Yet, to this day, I still feel like crying when I go to visit my country.

I feel uncomfortable with love; I have come to the conclusion that I simply don't know what it is to love...

I got divorced three years ago. In this country, my ex-husband used to be very loving with me. Despite the fact that I wasn't crying anymore and that I felt relieved, a part of me continued to feel lonely. My brother was here as well, but he had his children and his life revolved around other things. My ex gave me a place in his life and in his family. The relationship lasted a total of six years; four and half of marriage. He was a strange person, with sudden mood shifts...

I feel like a bad person when I yell at someone; when I answer in a wrong tone, with ego or arrogance. Even when I mistreat with an ill manner, like my mother did...with attitude...When I spoke with my husband I used an imperative tone. Once, I discovered that he had lied to me, and I felt such a rush of anger that I threw the remote control against the wall…It was as if time stood still…The whole thing left me frozen; I could have stopped and think, but I didn't. It seemed like madness to me. I have only felt that way with my mother!

The fear that I felt during my adolescence has become reactive... and the anger as well. I felt very angry from my mother's aggressions…but I couldn't detach from her waist! We were united through a link of insanity and schizophrenia.

My mother is a difficult woman. People see her in the streets and they run from her…they don't want to deal with her. My dad has been meaning to leave her for the past forty years! She yells; they don't enjoy together…Now she has dementia; it's a terrible situation. I grew up on the defensive with such a dysfunctional family. A few months ago she broke her left hand and I flew back to my country in order to help her; her craziness was more obvious than ever! I felt dizzy and I had panic attacks. When I came back home I felt like I was mourning…

My anger increased after I got divorced, but that's what I learned from mommy. I felt it the most when I was driving. A year and a half into the marriage, it imploded; I felt so unloved! By then, he had had an injury and was addicted to strong pain killers. The situation put a damper on a lot of beautiful things between us...His behavior ruined everything; he became dangerous!

Even so, I could have been a better wife and I could have related to him in a healthier manner.

I feel like a bad person when I act aggressively. My friends call me on it; I think even my co-workers! I am afraid of ridicule...I was so embarrassed by my parents!

Then, I had another relationship that went nowhere. I wanted to get serious, move on to the next level...He didn't. He didn't have a life's project; he's a momma's boy. I saw him again just to close that chapter. I spent a month in anguish; filled with insecurities. I felt alone in the world, like nobody loved me; I felt my lack of self-love...

I was so depressed that I didn't care about anything. It was so hard to be with myself that I sought refuge in work. Now, I work from eight in the morning until eight at night...I have no personal life... Before, I was yawning at three in the afternoon; now it's like, "finally, the night!" However, everything loses its purpose because I can't please anybody... I am exhausted and overwhelmed...Stop the world, I want to get off!

I feel more lonely than depressed; the loneliness overwhelms me... and the older you get, the less attention you get from men. I go through such situations when I leave home! Those who show some interest, later on they stop calling, hang up on me, and get lost…

I have no energy to wear a mask, so I isolate myself. Who wants to be with someone that lives in a constant state of anguish? I truly feel that all of this has to do with the way I am…I thought I had left my country trying to escape, because my mom is so crazy, because I couldn't breathe over there; but it turns out that now, I am just as crazy as her, or worse, and I can't even live here! My life is ridiculous. I have accomplished professional success, but, what good is it to me?

I am not married and I have no kids… No matter where I turn, I can't get a sense of direction…

I am too emotionally damaged!

## Sofia's Case Analysis

*Sofia seeks professional help at the apex of her loneliness and desperation. She has unfinished business with her country of origin, her family, her social and intimate relationships... However, she has many resources, even though she thinks she does not. Amongst some of those resources there is her capacity to realize that aggressiveness, just as cowardness, are both expressions of fear. She has also identified the source of her problems: the lack of self-love that has been faithfully reflected back to her through her parents.*

*She has succeeded in life because, contrary to her beliefs, she is intelligent and articulated. But she is extremely mental; her mind is her worse enemy! On top of that, she has done so much "therapy" throughout her life that she has become an informed patient; she lives diagnosing and self-diagnosing, turning every personal treat, or those of her family members, into pathologies.*

*It is true that everything seems to indicate the presence of some pathology in her parents, but the fact that she has chosen to continue to live according to, or in reference to them (specially her mother), is something dysfunctional in and of itself. One could think that it is just because she is a woman, given the fact that socially, women seem to revolve more around the home. But in these cases, it is the first born who tends to blame more the parents for their own dysfunctional behaviors, and as such, the family dynamics. It just so happened that Sofia's brother chose the centrifuge and, apparently, he is doing well...So, there has to be more to it!*

*Clearly, the villain of the movie is the mother; at least in Sofia's mind. In a black or white reality, the world is divided between good and bad people, but out inner psychic reality is far more complex than that. As soon as you start working with the "bad" parent, such as in a case like this, sooner or later the "good" parent also gets into trouble...*

*In her predicament, Sofia is blocking her couple aspect, which constantly brings her back to her childhood and the relationship between her parents.*

*It is interesting to note that the couples she speaks about are dysfunctional, childish, or unable to commit themselves; in other words, they are her imago. Inadvertently, Sofia is creating a reality based on her lack of affection; the snake that eats itself.*

*Clearly, she has pending issues to solve with her parents and it is imperative to deal with them as soon as possible (this is another innerving point to her: the passing of time). In the case of her mother, the pending issue has to do with her obvious personality disorder; but in the case of her father, it has to do with him being emotionally absent. This issue is completely omitted in Sofia's predicament because, after all, dad was there for her. But, it is one thing to have a male presence, and another is to have a functioning man in one's life. Her father is what is known as a tangential father; he is present, but does not perform.*

*If her father does not perform his duty as the man of the house, and her older brother leaves her, then...what kind of male role model did she have? A father provides, protects and establishes a model of what it is to be a man (as a couple). Therefore, since there is no man in Sofia's childhood or adolescence, it will be difficult for a man to be in Sofia's life as an adult, unless she becomes conscious of it.*

*Sofia also felt unprotected, which in turn makes her feel unworthy. Since she has never felt protected –more like exposed and ridiculed – she feels she has no worth.*

*She relates to others coming from that sense of unworthiness; be it friends, co-workers or couples. In her heart, she needs to reconcile her parents so she can accept in her mind that it is not her place to judge the way her parents are, nor the relationship that they have had. This also weighs in her lack of a couple... For as long as her feminine and masculine archetypes are quarreling, she will be incapable to attract and retain the couple that she wishes and deserves. This explains the way in which she ferociously attacks men that get involved with her – in whom she transfers– and then self-diagnoses herself as having a problem with uncontrollable rage.*

*There are several wounds considered to be primordial. In Sofia's case, she has suffered her mother's rejection...the first figure she was attached to. She is the most important person in her life, who she wishes to please at all costs. When she cannot do it, she gives into an insecure attachment just like her father...*

*Sofia has learned from her mother to reject others...and to reject herself. The issue here is that if her mother had continued to reject her for a longer period of time, Sofia would have completely*

pg. 58

*renounced her mother's love. However, because her mother's rejection was intermittent, the child received it occasionally (proof that her mother was capable of giving it), but she had no way to know when it would happen again!*

*Now, she systematically rejects as a precaution; for fear of being rejected. But because she rejects who she is, she also rejects any kind of help. This is how she punishes herself, sinking in her loneliness and pain...*

*Since the attraction factor in Sofia is that terror of being rejected, she manifests, among other things, a bulling teacher that ridicules her in front of the whole class; this is another form of rejection. Usually, a teacher is a person that teaches at many levels, not just academically, so we view their influence as something that exalts and illuminates. It is understood that they –teachers– are human, and because of that they can make occasional mistakes, since they may be going through some personal hardship; that is a part of life. Nowadays, when the phenomenon of bulling is well documented, it is important to bring to everyone's attention that it is not just the parents who may display disruptive behaviors toward children, but that teachers and other school personal may do so as well. In reality, bulling teachers have always existed...they abuse their power or their patronage. The presence of this bulling teacher in Sofia's life only adds to her psychological damage, by making her feel inadequate and unintelligent throughout her life. From this point on, the patient began to display somatization of her emotionally unstable states.*

*Anemia, according to the precepts of Bioneuroemotion, is a biological response to a wish to disappear from one's family. It points to a*

worthiness issue; a resentment that says: *"I am
under the impression that I am bothersome to my
family."* Or, *"I am drowning in this family."* It is the
*"place of no place"* of the psychoanalyst. By not
having a place in his birth family, she feels
abandoned, and she generalizes this feeling by
seeing that she does not have a place in the world...
This is the reason why she isolates herself and
harbors a passive wish for death.

Not only did Sophia not have a place, but she
also did not have someone to talk to throughout her
childhood; someone to answer her questions and
listen to her problems. This happens frequently, so
she speaks to herself; she asks and answers the
questions; she cries and comforts herself, until she
has so many voices in her head that she feels at the
edge of losing her mind. To top it off, her mother
inducted her into not trusting anyone, and because of
that, she blocked her desires and finally ended up
hiding in herself. At the same time, the anger and
resentment kept building up, for the more one tries to
repress something, the more it grows.

The client has also grown up with a conflict of
identity, which is why she does not know what her
project in life is. She needs to work with her inner
child in order to release those early created patterns
that need to change in order for her to be happy.
From the perspective of an adult, she can accept that
even though she was rejected in her childhood, she
does not necessarily want to say that her parents did
not love her. Her mother was probably rejected as a
little girl, and that is why she continues to reject
herself, and her father responds with a sense of
guilty externalized by his choice to continue to
struggle by staying with her mother.

*"The old saying: 'A healthy mind in a healthy body' should read instead: 'A healthy body in a healthy mind."*

Jorge A. León.

## Sofia's Action Protocol:

1. *Recognize that it is human to feel resentment when one suffers intensely and secretly as a child. Allow yourself to be angry when it appears that is the logical answer to any given circumstance, but do something constructive with it.*
2. *Admit that you never intended to end your life, but the judging and self-compassionate aspects of yourself.*
3. *Talk to your parents and express how you felt without pointing any fingers; accept them unconditionally and forgive them.*
4. *Forgive yourself for having loved so much a mother that caused you so much "damage," and a father who was "incapable of protecting you." Recognize your own worth,*

pg. 61

*and how brave you were to choose a set of parents that presented you with the challenges to own those aspects of your life.*

5. *Learn that when one gets away from a certain role model, one ends up living by it; and because you do not want to imitate it, give yourself permission to be yourself.*

6. *In your heart, reconcile your parents so that you can stop judging them in your mind. For as long as your masculine and feminine archetypes are in dispute, you will be incapable of attracting and keeping the person that you need to evolve as a couple.*

7. *Reconcile with your birth country (motherland) and with God (father).*

8. *Be understanding and compassionate with yourself, and do not fight your emotions; we are made to feel.*

9. *Listen to your intuition, rather than your altered ego.*

10. *Get in contact with your inner power and flow with life.*

# V

## "Oh Mother!"

*The story of Mirtha, 51 years old*

My premise in life has always been to be happy. However, ever since I can remember I have painful memories. "Life is not for the cowardly nor for the depressed," I used to say to myself in an effort to encourage me to keep going, but it took years to gather the courage to drive my mother out of my life, and inevitably, I became depressed. This is my story...

I had two wonderful grandparents that made me feel loved and special. My grandmother barely knew how to read and write, but she gave me all she could. Both left me too soon. My grandfather passed when I was 14 years old and shortly after, my grandmother lost her mind. Thank goodness God kept her alive for 3 more years, for if she had gone sooner, I would have died. I never thought ill of my mother until my grandmother died. At that moment, I realized that she was a monster.

A monster only chooses someone worse in an effort to look good; that was my father. He never gave me anything, but if by any chance he had a nice gesture toward me, she would tell me: "Don't think that he loves you; he is just crazy." When I went to school I met other families. Thank God, because it gave me a break, even if just for a few hours, from being around that toxic woman.

My mother tortured us all the time. She constantly repeated that I was responsible for her misfortune... What misfortune? What did she mean by that? She also derived a special sense of enjoyment from telling me that my father was a son of a bitch... At the time those words hurt; I suppose because I wondered what that said about me...

To my grandparents she said many awful things, even though they were like two angels. However, I never heard them speak ill of my mother or disown her. She didn't take pity on my grandmother when she was agonizing. In fact, I believe she poisoned her... And to her father, she literally pissed him off to the point of death. One day he was so fed up with her insults that he held a stick to hit my mother in the head. He managed to refrain from doing it, but he died the next day of a massive heart attack.

Little did I know her insults and ill-treatment would be my daily bread for years to come!

By the way, I don't know if she was a lesbian. When she divorced my father, she went around with a woman who never got married. Once she asked: "Do you know what your father has told me? That my friend and I are lovers; how dare he!" That same weekend she took me to a hotel, introduced me to the woman and left me there with her even though I was a minor. When I noticed that she wasn't coming back,

I left, although the woman insisted that I stayed and had a drink with her. I was just 17 years old! Sometime after that I realized what had happened: she tried to get me involved with the woman so that my father would stop being suspicious of her... That was my mother.

When I got married she used to say that my husband was disgusting. She'd throw things at him. My poor husband, the sweetheart that he is! Then, my daughter was born. How happy I was! One day I was so overjoyed that I thanked my mother for giving me life because it gave me the opportunity to be a mom. She didn't look at me, or said anything... I acted as if I didn't notice; I was so happy that all I could think of was my daughter.

Enthusiastic, I would leave work as fast as I could just to go and breast feed my baby. One day I came home and my daughter wasn't hungry: my mother had fed her! I asked her why she had done that, why couldn't she give her some water instead, knowing that I was about to arrive home. She yelled at me with a threat in her tone: "Don't you ever tell me what I have to do!" With pain in my soul and in my breasts, the thought of throwing myself in front of a running bus crossed my mind... I gave up breast feeding my baby girl.

Around the same time we had the opportunity to come to this country. To me, it was unthinkable to leave my mother alone; it was like turning my back on her. So, we brought her with us when we emigrated.

My mother could never speak ill of me back home because everybody knew me, but here, I noticed that some of our neighbors and friends began to reject me. Even she would show signs of disgust whenever I was around...

One day I noticed my mail has been missing. We went to the post office to find out what was happening, and we even filed a claim against a man that appeared to be suspicious... in lack of answers my husband and I hid to find out what was happening and I caught her. I thought I was losing it... I never could've imagined! How could she be so Machiavellian? I began to hide from her, in my own house! I would spend my life inside my room! That went on until I bought a beach apartment. I felt so happy away from her! On the second time that I went to spend the weekend at the apartment, I came back to my house to find shit smeared all over the floor...
On the brink of desperation, I went down on my knees and begged her for forgiveness. I didn't know what I could possibly have done, that was so horrible, to deserve been treated so badly, when my whole life was a constant and vain effort to make please her, to make her love me... She asked me to stop torturing her! "You know that I have a frail heart" she told me...After that, she went on living for another long 20 years.

She pulled the shit stunt several times. I don't know whether she would accumulate the feces in a container before spreading them or what, but whenever I would get home from the beach apartment the same mess would be there again... I was recently told by my daughter that once as a teenager, she saw that I was so tired that she didn't tell me about it and she alone cleaned the shit from the floor because she felt sorry for me. My daughter knew nothing of what I had lived with my mother...

Then my mother was diagnosed with bladder cancer and had two surgeries. After the first one, she seemed to be waiting for the right moment to jump on me. I have always been very intuitive. She was being brought in a wheelchair and tried to hit me. I jumped to avoid her punch but I sprained my right ankle and broke the left one. Then, I was also in a wheelchair... I became depressed, of course, I cried all the time. My daughter would come to me and ask me what was wrong, and I was so dumb that my only answer was, "nothing." Nobody knew of these things. It wasn't until much later in my life that I spoke about it.

However, I used to tell myself that I didn't have to feel that way. By then my daughter had just started university, I had a wonderful husband, a home... I found solace in my own way... but when she was released from the hospital, I took her back home. At that time, she gave me Judas' kiss, every day. I was in a wheelchair, yet I cleaned and ironed while she didn't move a finger. One day she snapped at my face: "Why do you always think of your husband and not of your mother?" Then I understood: all she felt was envy. That's why she attacked me! I felt such disgust in my heart...

After the second surgery it was obvious that she told the hospital personnel that I was a bad daughter and that I abused her. One day I caught her talking to a male nurse. He realized her intentions and contradicted her. I heard it all and right at that moment I entered the room. As if nothing had happened, she turns to me and tells me: "Come, sit here." I acted as if I had not heard a word before, to avoid confrontation, so I went to her. When I was in front of her she pulled the trigger: "You have always been abusive toward me, and right now you are abusing me!" For the first time I faced her, and what came out, I said it from the depths of my bowels... "I'm leaving the fuck out of here. Go and see who's going to take care of you, because I'm done with you!" My husband, who was right behind me, became inflamed like never before; and for the first time, he put her in her place. I had never seen him like that; never before, never again.

"I have to move on," I told myself, but that day I stopped loving her.

I had never been to a psychologist before, so I went to one. He wasn't a bad person, but on the third visit he asked me: "How could you have lived with a mother like that?" I knew then that he wouldn't be able to help me. So, I took it to hate psychology and psychologists... until I met you.

Nevertheless, the day my mother was discharged from the hospital, I was there again. "Am I stupid?" I asked myself. What was the first thing she said as she saw me? "I've always managed to get people to do as I please!" she said with a triumphant smile. I thought to myself: "I confronted her once and here I am so, never again!" Yet again, everything went back to the way it had always been...

When I turned 50 years old, my husband asked me: "Why don't you just get her out of the house once and for all?"
"Do you think I can?" I replied. "Of course you can!" he said. I rented a beautiful little study apartment overlooking a lake, and to my surprise, she agreed to move out! I hired a caregiver for her, because from then on I knew there was no turning back.

The day I drove her out of my house I felt such peacefulness! However, in my mind, something kept torturing me. How was it that I, being so strong, ended up being the abused one? How was it that I, the one who suffered, was able to act as if nothing was ever wrong? How did I allow her to do all these things to me?

A few days later I received a call, the caretaker was letting me know that my mother had fallen and was taken to the hospital. Then I learned that I was going to be sued for property damages. The proprietors asked me to go and see... as if I didn't know what I was going to find. I paid someone to go and clean soiled apartment... Oh mother! You devastated my life, you... disgusting swine!

I never really hated her. However, if I really search in my heart, I could never understand why she couldn't treat me with humanity, even though I always gave her the opportunity to do so...

She died in a hospice a year later.

I don't know why I had an internal debate on whether or not I should go to her funeral.
"If you are going to have a guilty conscience for not going, then go. If not, then don't go", said my husband.

I didn't feel guilty.

## Mirtha's Case Analysis

Mirtha lives according to *irrational beliefs*, which is why she feels like she can't go on, as if she has reached the limits of her strength. It is obvious: she cannot live up to what she preaches! How can she live with beliefs as: "My premise in life has always been to be happy" or "I have to keep on going, I can't stop"? If happiness is the goal, it will come with its share of unhappiness, because they are two sides of the same coin; there will be no pause in that emotional rollercoaster. One can only find peace by becoming self-aware.

What Mirtha ignores is that she carries a *program* that is not hers. Why is that obvious? Because like she said at the beginning of her narration, ever since she can remember, she had painful memories. This clearly indicates a *transgenerational* legacy of pain.

Since we do not know beyond the third generation, one must pay close attention to the grandmother. She probably conceived her daughter in some unwanted manner, or maybe the child turned out to be the unwanted gender. In some way, the grandmother must have looked at her daughter with perplexity, as a failed product; as a monster. Every child's primary objective is to obey their parents. If this is the mother's vision, she –the child– will unconsciously manifest that vision. To think of one's child as a blessing would be the equivalent to having a positive vision. But in this case, it is obvious that the child is considered to be a curse. Mirtha places herself in the polarity of her mother in order to repair that vision. She seeks to redeem her mother by trying to prove that she –the mother– is good, because Mirtha herself –the offspring– is good. Given that this is an unconscious mechanism, Mirtha sinks into denial of her mother's rejection and contempt, and as a robot, she accepts the unacceptable. This situation creates an inner conflict that drains her of her vital energy, and as the days goes by –like any other mistreated woman– she cannot find the way out of the *abuse cycle*.

From a symbolic *archetype* point of view, we are supposed to take nourishment from our mother, and because of that, Mirtha remains attached to her progenitor waiting to receive such sustenance. In turn, she only received toxicity. As an adult, her greatest dilemma is knowing that she will never receive that which her inner child innocently longs for. As a result, she feels devalued and behaves indecisively; she lacks the will power to act, or to change direction in life. When she finally makes a move towards independence by moving to the United States, in an act of supreme incoherence, she brings the mother with her.

Now the predator is in her territory, and the eagle pecks out Prometheus' liver, day after day...

One of the methods of systematic torture Mirtha's mother uses against the consultant is to slander her father. She fails to take responsibility for choosing him and getting pregnant as a result. She only resents that her life changed afterwards. She then hates her daughter, amongst other reasons, because she is the result of a relationship that she wishes to forget; the offspring of that man that she so despises. Now she has a *scapegoat*, someone that can carry the weight of everything that turned out to be wrong with her life. This is why she cannot stand her, nor can she stand to see her happy, either with her husband or her daughter. Her daughter is a painful remainder of her own unhappiness, so she becomes even more spiteful towards Mirtha.

According to most cultural standards it is clear that this lady did not love her daughter. This statement may be shocking for those who idealize the love of a mother, but to give birth does not make a mother out of a woman; just as donating semen does not make a father out of a man. What I want to emphasize is that a person who does not love herself cannot love anybody else, which is why this is such a crucial moment for Mirtha. According to *Family Constellations* it's a complete different story, because even in a twisted fashion, what Mirtha's mother felt for her daughter was love; period.

As Mirtha sinks into denial about her depression, she becomes obsessive which, coupled with her desire to please her mother beyond all logic, almost drives her mad... and at that moment she goes to get professional help. It is important to notice that she sought psychological help, but instead, she found someone who also needed help, because that person took her pain at a personal level, which rendered him incapable of providing her with the assistance she needed. To have a diploma on the wall, or a license to practice, does not mean that the psychologist, analyst or psychotherapist, is capable of helping a person, nor does it mean that it is the right person to help a specific client. Due to the intimate nature of the therapeutic relationship, our profession has a particularity, and that is, if the professional cannot help he/she will actually cause harm.

Yet, there is still an issue that was intently left lingering in the air: Was Mirtha's mother lesbian? Was she made to deviate from her sexual inclination or preference? Did she repress herself due to social convention, and in her frustration decided to take revenge on anyone she thought to be responsible for her suffering? We will never know. However, this is not the topic of discussion. The paternal role should not rest on the parent's sexual preference or level of sexual satisfaction.

Now, the question that the client faces is the following: Is it acceptable for a daughter to abandon her mother? For the longest time, Mirtha could not fathom the idea of doing such a thing. She made a *childhood decision* to prove that she was a good person, different from her mother and at the same time trying to demonstrate to her mother that she was a good daughter, different from her father. Any child wishes to know that they are the son or daughter that their parents dreamed of, but this effort renders Mirtha with an identity crisis. Her primal role models are not to follow and her "good" role models, her grandparents, are mostly characterized by passivity and submissiveness, traits very present in Mirtha's behavior.

Let us review an incarnation through a set of parents whose souls have a *vibrational affinity* to ours. Expressing the ignorance of this truth through dissatisfaction, may lead one to believe in the illusion that it is possible to be different from our parents by just putting distance in between. But that which we hate the most about our parents is exactly what resonates with us, and when we suppress it or deny it, it becomes part of our *shadow*; poorly qualified energy seeking resolution. It is the Frankenstein, the Mr. Hyde, or the "evil voice" that we need to accept and integrate in order to release all the energy that we have been using to suppress it. As we do this, all that energy becomes available to us. When we love and integrate our dark side (the force), everything in life becomes brighter. The sense of struggle end as we stop trying to fix ourselves, and instead we begin to flow with life. For those who still believe in karma, let us think that karma is everything we have yet to learn, and that whenever we are ready, it presents itself... no more, no less.

Mirtha does well to leave her mother; the problem is that she never let her go. She sought out psychotherapy because she knows that unless she lets her go, she will undoubtedly repeat the same story of sadness and maternal frustration. Except in this case, it would be a modern version of it.

One should leave a mother that behaves like this. It is not about abandoning her, but there is no need to bring her along. Love a mother like this from the heart, but sever daily interaction to cut her tentacles in order to prevent her from causing more harm. No drama or guilt trips. Not all mothers are good, and not all mothers know how to express love to their children.

*"What is left from yesterday, is my executioner today."*

Deepak Chopra

## Mirtha's Action Protocol:

1. *Understand that, as a soul, you chose this mother as a reminder to not disrespect yourself. It is a hard lesson which, evidently, you did not conquer on a previous incarnation.*
2. *Feel compassion for your mother and forgive her; this is the beginning of your true healing.*
3. *Take personal responsibility and accept that, after all, your mother was not such a terrible person; on the contrary, she supported you through the hardest lesson that you needed to learn; self-love. Stop acting through a false concept of love, which is merely the lack of love for yourself.*
4. *Forgive yourself for having cared so much for your mother, and so little for your own self.*
5. *Since your mother has already passed, write her a letter. Keep it until the next day and read it out loud, as if your mother was in front of you, then burn it immediately after. Be very*

conscious as you do this exercise, and let the fire burning be like a ceremony. Once you externalize the unbalanced emotions, you will have rid yourself of them, forever.

6. Honor your mother. She mirrored your lack of self-love. You will realize that deep inside there was nothing to forgive; you both were characters of a play in this illusion we call life.
7. Recognize the bitterness that you exerted during all these years, and consciously begin to project love to everyone and everything.
8. Love and enjoy yourself... you are a person of great worth! Start a diary of appreciation and count your blessings every day.
9. Open yourself to receive all the happiness that you have denied yourself up until now. You deserve all the good life has reserved for you.

# VI

## "I refused maternity"

*The story of Gabriela, 60 years old*

I was married for twenty years. I didn't want to have children because I liked to party. I had an abortion before giving birth to my only child, and then another one after. My daughter was a planned child, because I was really happy during that time of my life. I barely ate... I took so much care of my body that I was 6 months into the pregnancy by the time the belly started showing. I spent 12 hours in labor, for various circumstances. When they realized I wasn't dilating and the baby was losing her pulse, they decided to perform a C-section; thank God, because the umbilical cord was tied up around one of her arms...She was born with a cone head and really, really hungry!

Her father left me for a tourist woman. He wanted to go to her country, so he divorced me as fast as he could. I told him: "If you want to leave, I want full custody." He agreed, but left me in debt and misery. Obviously, he ended up regretting his decision and tried to come back, but I didn't want to; to me, his betrayal was too great. My father was very ill back home and I went back to be with him during his last moments. During that time, he left his own daughter at some friends' house so he could disappear with the woman. When I came back, I didn't even know where my daughter was! It was very hard... Then, he would promise to come and visit her and he wouldn't show up. My daughter had a real hard time with it. He claims to love her, but he doesn't come to see her. Every now and then he'll call me and tell me that I am the love of her life, and that he would kill for me...what good is that for me?

When we separated I started to go out; to discos, parties...everywhere. I would leave the girl with my sister and go out and live. She realized that my daughter was all nervous, eating a lot; not well at all...but that didn't stop me.

During that time I met a very good man. I became calmer with him; I didn't go to bed late and I barely drank...I was a housewife. But then, the inevitable happened... What a disappointment! To think that my daughter loved him as a father...but he hurt her...I never would have thought that he could do something like that... I never doubted my daughter's word. When I told the man that he would have to leave the house because of what had happened, he asked me: "How could you think that I would do something like that?" But he didn't deny it! It was the last I heard of him, because just as I drove him out of my house, I also drove him out of my life...

Around that time I developed a strange auto-immune disease, and because of the medicine I take I have inflammation all over my body. To think that I was so pretty! I can't say why, but I haven't had any more relationships. Sometimes I think that was my last chance, but I don't regret it; everything happened the way it did and I haven't had a partner since…

Now, my only concern is my daughter.

She gets with some men that are like…gosh! She says she doesn't feel pretty and I don't understand why; maybe if she had some sort of physical malformation or something of the sort…but no, she is a completely normal girl.

Before I used to go out, but not anymore…I live in a constant state of concern about her! I don't know what else she needs; she has everything to be happy, but she's depressed!

Every now and then she'll come up with the idea that she wants to die. I took her to see a nontraditional medicine man, the Christian church, a witch doctor… I don't know what else to do with her…She needs urgent therapy!

## <u>Gabriela's Case Analysis</u>

Gabriela is a good example of the prototype of one who is "more of a woman, than a mother." In fact, even though she wishes to have her baby, she is more concerned by the looks of her body than the nutrition of the baby growing inside of her. Then, she makes fun of it by saying that her baby was born being hungry...The baby girl that she brought to the world was already born with a program of death –expressed by the umbilical cord twisted around her arm– and because of that, the labor was dangerous and difficult.

The client is also filled with an incoherence that identifies the daughter as the patient, when in fact her daughter is a mere carrier of the family dysfunction.

There are people who cannot understand –hence, insist on denying– that children carry the absent couple within themselves. The "absent" parent is well alive and active in the blood, the memories and the energetic field of the child. Moreover, every couple –temporary or not– that the custodian partner shares with, becomes a part of the soul of the family; if it isn't a good choice, the most fragile member of the family will express it one way or another (discordantly, of course), given that it is the most sensitive within the group.

*Gabriela also speaks about her divorce, and subsequent dissolution of the family with a coldness that is appalling; and she does the same when she speaks about the illness of her daughter. The experience with her second partner seemed to have been more disturbing than the first one, but it is not clear if it is due to her daughter, or herself. What is clear is that she is somaticizing, as well as her daughter, although the latter expresses her lack of worth and self-esteem in different ways.*

*Gabriela's auto-immune condition is the physical manifestation of her self-punishment programming; because of her abortions, her inability to choose a good partner, for having neglected her daughter, for her inability to communicate with her, for whatever. She desperately seeks for love, but a different kind than the one she has received so far... just like her daughter.*

*She has also developed an aversion to men that she projects on her daughter, which is why she disapproves of her boyfriends. Until Gabriela decides to bring a solution to her own traumas, she will continue to watch her daughter treading on a road of unhappiness that will be even deeper than her own.*

*Gabriela has a hard time adapting to new circumstances, which is the reason life keeps presenting her with new opportunities to do so, again and again, in order for her to learn that lesson! Nonetheless, she focuses in her daughter so she can prove that she is a good mother that "worries," and even "sacrifices" herself for the good of her daughter. She wishes to impress her daughter, but because the effort is imposed and out of time, she ends up overwhelming her.*

*The concerns that Gabriela has for her daughter are only a reflection of what is happening inside of her. She would do well to seek counseling for herself, for as she insists on using her daughter as the escape goat, she continues to compromise her daughter's mental, emotional, physical and spiritual health; and in the end, Gabriela's predicament will continue the be unresolved. To reshape one's self and become coherent is the work of a healthy, functional, independent and joyful being, and that is the best legacy that she can leave to her daughter.*

*"The reflection of the parents is manifested on their children; only by improving that reflection will the infinite light of the creator be manifested in the form of changes"*

Chico Xavier

## Gabriela's Action Protocol:

1. *Identify all the situations and people in your life toward whom you feel hostility, but at the same time continue to seek their approval.*
2. *Allow yourself to feel the grief for the two pregnancies that you ended, and forgive yourself; only then, will you clean yourself and all your relations from that energy.*
3. *Stop looking for approval or recognition. Realize that you do not need to get sick in order to have the attention of your loved ones. This will in turn allow your daughter to stop seeking attention through negative behaviors, which is what she has learned from you so far.*
4. *Quit being so hard on yourself and everybody else; do not judge or criticize. Learn to see with the eyes of the heart.*
5. *Give yourself the right to ask for what you want. If others do not answer to your*

pg. 83

expectations, do not be disappointed...no body owes it to you!

6. Accept that you cannot change any body, including your daughter, and instead, invest your energies in transforming your life at all levels.

7. Do your best to not hold grudges and bitterness against any one; specially avoid feelings of revenge. If you experience any of these feelings, allow them to come like waves in the ocean. In any case, do not suppress them; look for creative and edifying ways to use these powerful feelings.

8. Allow yourself to grieve for all your losses. Recognize and resolve them, and assimilate what you have learned. Get over them, once and for all!

9. Review the fears that arise in you because of your daughter, and resolve them; they are a mirror of what is happening inside of you.

10. Show appreciation to your body, instead of criticizing it or thinking that it is defective because it is manifesting an illness, or "ugliness"; your daughter will end up doing the same.

11. Give yourself the right to experience pleasure, consciously focusing on all the good things in your life.

# VII

## "A lot of weight on my shoulders!"
*The Story of Ashley, 17years old*

I just want to die. I get panic attacks and I can't breathe. I feel that I good for nothing, and that I am not loved. I see everything in negative. I don't like anything about my life, nothing! I don't even like my name… it's such a common name. I don't change it because otherwise people wouldn't know who I am…

Every day, I take four pills: for depression, anxiety, panic attacks and sleeping…

My mother told me that I was born with the umbilical cord wrapped around my neck, and that my father passed out during the delivery; I don't know whether he did out of fear, or disgust…

I have been told that I look like an aunt who died of cancer in the stomach at a very young age. I would have liked to have known her; I am told that she was controversial, because she did whatever she wanted. Once, there came a lady to visit us, and she compared the two of us in a very specific manner;, but I noticed that my parents didn't seem to want her to talk about those things in front of me, or elaborate on the details, so I was kicked out of the room. To this day I remember the expression on her face, for she seemed to be in a trance…

My life has a clear 'before' and 'after'; my parents separated when I was five years old, and then divorced a year later. He used to yell a lot at my mother: "Whore," he called her. She says that was not true, but I remember it. He re-married a year later and has another daughter. My dad has been a piece of trash…I haven't seen him in years…

Before the separation, I was always with the two of them: then, with none. My mother left me alone all the time and I thought she didn't love me, because love is supposed to be expressed through actions. It is assumed that a person that loves you, cares for you, gives you affection and takes precautions for you…

I have difficulty hugging people; even my family. I am easily influenced by others because I am highly empathic, but sometimes I can be very cold… My friends tell me: "You only have one face!" because I always have the same facial expression...

If something is wrong, I always find a way to make it my fault... It's happened to me so many times! And after feeling sad, I only feel emptiness...It's hard to explain. I am very perceptive of energies, but I feel trapped in my own body. I am also kind of emotional and jealous of anybody who has more than I do. More than anything I am helpful; the problem is that I hide my sadness...

I have never been satisfied with myself, with relationships, and not even with friendships. When I was eight years old I had a crush on a boy, but he said ugly things to me because I wasn't like my friend, whom he really liked; he was very persistent with her, however, my friend didn't pay attention to him.

From that moment on I began to feel ugly. On top of that, since I turned ten years old my mother used to tell me: "You were born hungry," because I ate too much, but she didn't notice that I also drank a lot of water and peed a lot. When I turned eleven I was diagnosed with type II diabetes...

After that, my mother had a boyfriend who sexually molested me. I was thirteen years old, as it was the year that I got my period for the first time...

My mother dumped him, but I suspect that she secretly resents having lost him because of me.

Then I went to high school, and I was bullied because I had pimples on my face, I was fat and ugly. I am 50/50; my mother's physical appearance and my father's character.

My first sexual encounter happened during a sweet fifteen cruise. After that, I slept with a boy from another school. My mom didn't like him because he didn't work, so she thought he was a good for nothing who would only drag me down; but I stuck with him because I felt that he truly loved me...

Now I have a constant relationship with mother, but it is one of control and manipulation. She says, "I am sad; I live for you" It's not fair! It bothers me, and besides, she judges way too much.

I usually lack motivation, feel tired and isolated; I don't want for anybody to see me. If death was an option, I would take it.

I feel selfish with my mom because I'm her only daughter and she doesn't have a couple. I am –more or less– the only person that she has in this world, but that feels like a weight that is too heavy on my shoulders!

pg. 88

## Ashley's Case Analysis

*When a fetus in the mother's womb has had the umbilical cord wrapped around their body, he will register in his brain the idea that to be autonomous entails a risk of death, because the moment that fetus is about to be born, it is also faced with the fact that it will die if it leaves the womb. So, this is how Ashley comes to us, expressing –in her adolescence– a difficulty to reclaim a space of autonomy in the presence of her mother.*

*In her father's case, the work is to help her recognize the fact that she has never had a father in the strict sense of the word, because her father behaved –and continues to behave – more like a distant uncle...*

*To heal the relationship with her mother will require more than an act of psychomagic, because Ashley perceives her mother as something ominous, to the extent that the latter seeks to compensate for what she did not do in its rightful moment. Besides, she also exhibits a typical adolescent's behavior in which the person is almost an adult, but lacks the inner power to face a parent that does not allow her children to grow.*

It would be good if the patient's mother realized that the only way to keep a child at home forever is by disabling his/her ability to live life. That saying that goes "mothers know best," is an obsolete paradigm.

Ashley feels diminished and useless in the face of her mother —who is more of a wonder woman— and she doubts herself and her capabilities. As a result, she feels ashamed and sad, which in turn leads her to isolate herself and feel pity for her own suffering. The situation makes Ashley wish to put an end to all of her suffering, but she mistakes that desire with a wish to end her life. In other words, she wishes for the death of who she has been, for she intuitively feels that there is another part of her that could achieve great things in this world.

Diabetes points to a lack of proper emotional nutrition. There is an underlying feeling of separation and/or disgust (same one she projects toward her father). In my experience, a person that suffers from diabetes is very sweet, but their "sugar" has become bitter. According to the Bioneuroemotion precepts, this condition has an undercurrent of resentment due to a "divided home." Lise Bourbeau says that child diabetes "manifests in a kid that does not feel properly acknowledged. The sadness from feeling this way creates a feeling of emptiness inside, which prompts the child to overcompensate. This is a way of seeking attention." All of the above apply to Ashley.

In any case, Ashley, about to turn eighteen, needs to acknowledge her victimization, open her *wings and go and live her life independently from what her parents have done in the past.*

*This is what is known as differentiation; the ability to take the best from one's birth family and shake off the rest, so that one does not go through life seeking approval and acceptance of others. Or, in the case of analytical psychology, the principle of individuation, so that Ashley may become an integral being.*

*The possibility that Ashley is exhibiting what Dr. Salomon Sellam describes as the "Yaciente" Syndrome, a replacement child syndrome, deserves special mention. The key is in her feeling that she is "trapped inside her own body," the "resemblance" with her diseased, "controversial" aunt, the "inability to hug," and who knows what else... even her wish to die...*

*It is clear that Ashley is the groundbreaker in her family, in a way that she was born with a mission (self-chosen) to break with the old and toxic ways of her genetics, and to find inside herself the strength to do it. This is the only chance she has to unleash the potential to live a wonderful life.*

*"At some point, the emerging of the new will converge and a new world will be born"*

Barbara Marx Hubbard

## Ashley's Action Protocol:

1. *Make a paper or cardboard coffin. Fill it with hay or wood shavings and bury it wherever suits you. This will bring closure to your relationship with your father and you will stop resenting his abandonment.*
2. *Do a relaxation exercise visualizing both your parents, each with its own inner struggles, contradictions and unfulfilled dreams... Feel compassion toward them and forgive them.*
3. *Know that you do not need to take care of your mother, or protect her; just honor her (this also means not judging her).*
4. *Admit that you have a tendency to exaggerate things because of your great sense of fear and the suffering that you went through as a child...resolve it! If you continue to re-create*

*the old, you will prevent new things from coming into your life.*

5. *Give up on allowing your, and others' excessive thinking to influence your life.*
6. *Stop believing that you are a cold person; find out what it is that prevents you from hugging someone else, because your choice of a couple (to this day) is no more than the outer expression of your inner desire to give and receive at the emotional level.*
7. *Forgive yourself for having felt unable to show your real strength. From today on, express your –very rich– inner world.*
8. *Realize that you already have everything you need to choose a new life, for your inaction has been a way of hurting yourself.*
9. *Accept your mission as part of those that will spawn a new type of humanity, and choose to take on a leading role. What you have lived so far has been part of your training to lead others. If you stop, it will be a source of trauma for you; if you step beyond the threshold of your fear, it will become your initiation.*

# VIII

## "I've never been so tragic"
### *The Story of Camila, 59 years old*

When it comes to my daughter, I feel helpless; she is never on time to her commitments, never finishes what she starts… I say to her: "You have a monster that is in your imagination. You will only be able to live if you face it." I explain to her, in every way I can, that the only thing that matters in life is to be happy…without harming anyone, of course. But, come on! The more I try to get closer to her, the more she mistreats me. She has a special relationship with me, but only when she feels like crying; then she seeks me out! Her father says that I treat her as if she was crazy. I just want to feel that she loves me. I put on any pretext to call her; I need to know that she is well. I am not very trusting, but I also need to know that she cares about me. I give her everything. "You have to fight," I say to her, because I don't yell at her or offend her. I give her good advice. "Never get involved with a married man!" But she's a lost cause! Nothing good sticks to her...

She is the kind of person that goes to a psychologist, but I am not. She likes alternative therapies and all that kind of stuff. She wanted me to go with her to some sort of cabana in order to sweat and perform some ceremony. "I have no time for that," I told her... I am not into any of that! Then, she told me that she prayed for peace in the family, or something like that.

I have given a lot of affection to my daughter, because that is what I lacked in my upbringing; the story of my relationship to my mother is not a happy one... I have erased a lot of memories. My husband says that I forget everything. I have never been such a tragic person; these are things that my daughter doesn't know about me, and she doesn't have to know it!

From the day my daughter was born, she behaved with the force of three children. I couldn't go visit anyone because she would lose her patience and misbehave. I didn't care about it; instead, I would take her to the park. To me, my daughter was like having been given a second chance in life to be happy. As soon as she entered school she was diagnosed with ADHD.

Around that time I had a spontaneous miscarriage. I didn't know that my daughter was really looking forward to having a brother! She said repeatedly: "When my little brother is born, who will you love the most?" I would say to her: "Both," but she kept asking, until one day I told her: "Which leg do you love the most?" Only then did she stop asking. When I had the miscarriage I had to explain the situation to her, because she was driving me crazy planning for the arrival of the baby; "Your little brother got sick and went to heaven." She cried hard over the loss of her brother! However, she didn't talk to me about it; she expressed her feelings at school…

Due to the particular conditions in my country at the time, I couldn't study what I wanted. When my daughter became a lawyer I felt really happy: I felt that I had realized myself through her! "I accomplished what I wanted," I thought to myself. I was also happy for her, of course. I have always told her: "I want you to have a profession so that you get married for love." I don't want to hear her saying later in her life that she feels like a professional failure; even more, I don't want to hear her saying that she got into a bad marriage just for money!

I have blackmailed her into doing two things: I asked her to learn French, and I asked her to finish her law studies. She wanted to enlist in the Peace Corps! But I would have none of that; she has to achieve all the happiness that I never have! However, a little after she began working in her professional field she told me that she didn't like her profession, and that she preferred to do something that would be good for all of humanity… "Then you chose the perfect career!" I told her…and I thought that she had listened to what I had said…No way! A few days ago she told me – as if nothing – that she's going to go to medicine school. Medicine! And her father and I still carry a huge debt on her student loan! I was astounded… I never thought I could be that way… I never allowed my mother to hurt her! As soon as I regained my composure I was able to explain to her the reason I had such a reaction, and I also apologized to her. I know how to acknowledge my errors and shortcomings…

She hasn't called me in days... She is very special! It is a pain for me, and for her. I don't want anything; all I want is for her to look at me with some measure of love in her eyes. "Stop telling her what to do," my husband tells me. He says that I push her further away with my attitude, but in the end, he knows that I am right, and that I give her tasks that she can accomplish... Is just that I am too impatient!

Sometimes I think about adopting; I have so much love to give! I don't know if I am doing right. I feel that I have always damaged what I love the most. I need to resolve this.

She has to close this vicious circle of sacrifice!

# Camila's Case Analysis

*Camila certainly loves her daughter more than herself, because in reality she does not love herself at all. This is why her love is so conditional. She does not realize it, but her lack of affection is such that —evidently due to the lack of maternal love— she feels that her daughter has to fill that void. Obviously, her husband does not want to contradict her, but in that, he does not help her to grow and get out of the victim role that she so likes to adopt...*

*This mother has a great dilemma: she wants for her daughter to spread her wings and fly, to succeed, but she wants her to do this while keeping her tied up with two ropes: to recognize her mother, as well as, to be eternally grateful to her. She expects her daughter to do all the things that she did not... but at the same time she complains when the daughter attempts to go away. Camila threatens her with all sorts of dangerous scenarios so that she won't leave; but deep inside she blames herself, because she intuitively knows that in order to keep her daughter from leaving, she will have to somehow disable her abilities to live life on her own... as a result, she punishes herself.*

*In her desperation, Camila uses the sacrifice theme as a blackmail; a poor relative of true love, which is complete acceptance of the other, just as* he/she is. In her frustration, she substitutes the notion of sacrifice for another poor relative of true love: preoccupation. In order to sustain a position of preoccupation, there has to be a consistent and permanent source of danger; this is her daughter's curse...

Through the expression of her irrational beliefs, Camila not only turns life into a struggle, but she herself turns into a burden that her daughter refuses to assume. She does not relate to her daughter as a mother, but as a little girl that lacks parental love and wishes for her daughter to adopt her. Then again, she causes her daughter to pull away; not as if she is rejecting Camila, but rejecting the role reversal. A child is never a parent; because of this, her daughter pulls away just in time. However, Camila cannot see herself, and instead, she continues to project on her daughter...

Camila allows her daughter to go out to the world, but with an instruction's manual written through the filters of her own emotional lack. If her daughter was internalizing these instructions, she would not be able to freely experiment with, and live her own life. Since the father takes an opposite side to the mother, the daughter has a range of action that allows her to get close and pull away as she sees fit, and in accordance to her own needs and wishes. That range of freedom breaks the client's box in a way that plunges her into despair...

Therefore, comparison becomes Camila's secret weapon. When she feels cornered, she retaliates; but the moment she can establish a parallelism between her own mother and her daughter, she becomes her mother, because she does the exact same thing that her mother would... In this, her Mr. Hyde is *manifested; the shadow from which her daughter runs.*

*Camila does not know of motherly love and it is obvious that all of her efforts to please her mother were in vain. That didn't work out, so that dynamic stayed in her mind as "the" way in which a mother and daughter are to relate, and with that, she holds the expectation that her daughter will do anything to please her. It seems that in the past her daughter used to act according to her expectations, trying to make her mother happy through her own life, but she gave up when she realized that it was an impossible endeavor. Times have changed! As a result, she began to systematically pull away from her mother, eliciting a deep state of anguish in her. Now the sense of sacrifice that Camila used to feel seems to have been in vain as well, because it does not push a button in her daughter; she interprets this response as a lack of appreciation that she does not dare to express openly. She perceives her daughter as a selfish person, with no regard for her mother's "needs."*

*She fails to look in the mirror, and learn from a teacher that is giving her a great lesson of life... to be free!*

*"We enter the sunset of our lives completely unprepared for it. The worse part of it is that we go into it under the false assumption that our truths and ideals will be of any help at that stage."*

Dr. Wayne Dyer

## Camila's Action Protocol:

1. Go in search of your (inner) wounded child, give her a chance to heal and be with her as she grows to be your current age. She needs you as much as you need her!
2. Identify the unresolved issues with your own mother, and resolve them; it is interfering with your life.
3. Get rid of the sense of guilt that you continually project on your daughter.
4. Recognize that it is a delirium to pretend to know what is best for your daughter; she is her own being.
5. Become aware that your daughter's reactions are directly proportional to your insistence in

*making her responsible for satisfying your lack of affection.*

6. *Recognize that your daughter is an adult and begin to relate to her in a healthier manner.*

7. *Allow yourself to learn from your daughter and walk on the same path towards evolution. Celebrate and enjoy the privilege of being her mother!*

# IX

# "Bad investment!"

*The story of Marcela, 44 years old*

My parents divorced when I as one year old and he went to another country. Sometime later, my mother got involved in a relationship with a man that lasted about seven years. He was an alcoholic and abuser, but in his own way, he loved me very much. One time, I believe as attempts to infuriate my mother, he told her that as soon as she'd leave for work he was going to rape me... I was ten years old... Instead of leaving him, or calling the police, she wrapped me up like a package and sent me "on vacation" to my father's for three months. I ended up living with him for a year; the worse year of my life!

Obviously, I only took summer clothing with me. Autumn came and went; winter came and went, but I continued to wear the same summer clothes and nobody cared! How irresponsible! All because of my step mother's wickedness and my father's indifference toward me.

This is the same kind of men that I attract...how awful!

When that relationship finally ended, I went back to live with my mother. My life with her was even worse; every day she wanted to end her life because she didn't have a couple. She would open the gas line or sallow whole bottles of pills... Just about anything! I had to run all around after her thinking that her death would be the worst thing that could ever happen to me... how silly I was! This is how I spent my entire adolescence and the earlier stage of my life as a young adult: with my mother's craziness, her menopause and her dramas.

She was also aggressive...very! One day she grabbed me by the hair and spun me around. I was so beside myself that I decided to go live on my own, even though the inflation rate at the moment was of 400% in my country. The experiment didn't last very long though, but not because of me. She lost her job and I had to go back because I was the one with a job, of course! ... And so, I began to support her.

Sometime after, I began to date a young man who turned out to be the love of my life. The first time we slept together I fell asleep and got back home at 5:00 am in the morning. My mother slapped me as soon as I got to the door; she called me all sorts of names. He faced her, and said to her: "Lady, don't speak to her like that, please..." She interrupted him in the middle of the sentence and told him, "You are a man and I congratulate you for that. This is how you treat the kind of whore that she is." He answered to her: "She is not a whore, she is your daughter! And I love her." He was the only one to ever put her well where she belonged, and he did it with respect. Either way, she gave him an ultimatum, and for several months he couldn't even come near the front of my house…

Later on I had an abortion; not because of him, but because of my mother. I imagined myself having to go to work and leaving the baby in her charge. I made my choice and decided that I'd much rather carry the weight of my conscience for the rest of my life, before doing such a thing to a baby!

He was my companion, and I lost him in a motorcycle accident. Sometimes I imagine as if he is still with me… I see him naked, with a little belly… Then, I think that maybe I wouldn't have known how to value him, or that our relationship would have become a monotone. Who knows? Maybe I wouldn't have grown up doing certain things that I had to do because I was alone… I don't know; the thing is that I felt a terrible emptiness. I had the physical pain of not being able to hold his hand, and not having someone that would have my back! I was in so much pain, yet nobody ever noticed. The pain of his loss was so strong that I had to leave the country. But the pain came with me…

That was twenty one years ago. I made my way in this country on my own. When I was established, my mother showed up without even asking for permission. She said, "I'm coming to live with you," And she came. We started a business and it went broke. As I was financially stable I began to support her… again!

I made good money working as a masseuse at a luxury hotel. However, I wasn't very intelligent when it came to managing it. I had some fabulous years, but then I hurt my hands. During that time I had a health insurance that covered all the expenses and treatments. Once they said they couldn't keep paying for my expenses, I went back to work; the sacrifice was too great. Shortly after I had to stop working again; it was the bills or my health.

I found some work at a local government office, but I hated that job. Every day, I would lock myself in the bathroom to cry with a friend. The vibes where so low! All gossip and back stabbing... I couldn't stand it anymore so I quit the job; the drama was getting me sick. I had the luxury of quitting, but now I feel like a dirt bag; I am being overrun by guilt and worry...

In the meanwhile, my mother found an apartment y left me; now she lives better than me. She is a shameless leach. I feel used by her, by my friends and by men. I haven't spoken to her for over a year and I really couldn't care less...she sucked all my energy, and nothing as ever enough; never showed any appreciation or gratefulness. She stretched me to thin!

However, I feel guilty and that makes me feel even angrier; I should be able to process all of this!

Just today she called me, but I didn't answer the phone; I am not going to screw my day. She knows that I am not well and she wants to take advantage of the situation. Whatever favor I did to other people, she pretends that I should do the same for her! I tried to do Ho'oponopono but I couldn't. So, I went to see my dog. Sometimes I have to pretend in front of my "daughter" so she doesn't worry about me. One day I took her to the park and I was torturing my mind going about money issues... she came to a sudden stop, turned around and looked me straight in the eyes. I knew she was begging me to stop going about things in my head!

Sometimes I don't recognize my own self. I have no strength. My anxiety is more of the mind type; I never feel prepared for anything...ever! As if I had this voice in my head telling me: "Don't be so quiet." And then it may also say: "People don't understand." It happens very often.

Lately I also lost my car and now I have to take the bus...

I am very tired and I feel so alone. I tried to apply self-compassion, but this whole struggle makes no sense!

Now I am forty four years old and I have nothing. I busted my chops working; I didn't take good care of myself and never valued my own money. I continue to expose myself to futureless relationships. To this day, all my efforts have been nothing but a bad investment!

## Marcela's Case Analysis

*Marcela has hurt her hands because, unconsciously, she refuses to continue doing things against her will; be it working in something that she does not like and/or use the fruits of her labor to sustain her own predator: her mother. Hurting herself has given her the opportunity to stop doing that which takes her away from the purpose and mission that her soul has set for her. Her body gave her several warnings that she was over doing it, but she was too busy listening to the voices in her disintegrated mind... She went over board because she is running a self-destruction program.*

*The client harbors a lot of anger. Her story begins with the tale of her parents' divorce, and then, in her conscious mind there is nothing that allows for the recovery of what happened prior to that episode of her life. The relevance of this one event demarks the beginning of the fragmentation of her psyche...*

*Marcela's essence has "died" several times in her life. A part of it died of cold in a foreign country, which represented the irresponsibility of some parents who emotionally abandoned her; this is a programming conflict. Note how she speaks of herself as a "thing" when she relates that she was "wrapped and sent away like a package." By feeling that she was an object, she perceives that she has been treated as less than a human; feeling that comes to the surface from time to time, and which is also part of the ill treatment she feels coming from her parents (and that she expects from others). Another part of her chose to die over the tomb of the love of her life; this is the conflict which set the ball into motion.*

*She says her anxiety is of the mind because Marcela is such a mental person. Because she did not have anyone to answer her questions during her childhood, she asked and answered the questions herself, believing that the answers she gave herself were right. Today, she lives according to those beliefs, which have her wallowing in a pool of victimization...*

*In any case, Marcela is quite capable of becoming aware, for when she describes her father she realizes that she attracts the same kind of men into her life. It makes sense; it is her association of what a man is supposed to be. But even with all of that, when she blames her step mother she still justifies her father by saying that he was just being "indifferent." By "rescuing" him like that, she creates a trend in her life, for she will continue to rescue other adults behind their backs and with that, she will perpetuate the consequences of it. By justifying, she exonerates all men, but that only makes her despise (deeply) her own gender... and as such, herself.*

*Her first feminine role models bear the qualifications of "irresponsible," "evil," "crazy," and "aggressive." When she came back from the foreign country lacking for love and looking for her mother's support, she finds instead an immature woman who is making all sorts of suicidal attempts because she does not have a man in her life... As a result, Marcela postpones her own emotional needs in order to rescue her mother, and in doing so, she becomes a "parent-child," in other words, she becomes the head of the family.*

*This might have been the reason she chose not to have children of her own... She had already done it! She blames her mother and one could almost think that it is due to the mother's cruelty and madness, however, Marcela does not even contemplate the possibility of leaving with the "love of her life" and having her child somewhere else. No; she much rather giving up the product of her love and toss it away. This could be one explanation, but here is another one: Her mother/daughter is a reality, and she could never abandon her! In fact, she never did and that is a big chunk of her anger. When she finally created an unconscious opportunity for her mother to reciprocate all of her efforts (by taking care of her health), and even if it wasn't at the appropriate time, her mother chose to leave and take care of her own life, leaving her –once more– on her own!*

*In her childhood, Marcela reached the understanding that if nobody loved her it was because she was not a lovable person. It was a childish reasoning, but deep inside her being that paradigm continues to create her reality. This is why she does not honor her body and has commissioned it for demolition...that is how she feels... like she is falling apart!*

*Another source of resentment and preoccupation is money; she personifies money and says that it "tortures" her. Besides, she has an association that in order to make money she has to break her back for it. Since she has already done that, now she does not have any other option but to be poor, which diminishes her even more because she cannot find someone to sustain her through it all. Obviously, this does not mean that Marcela is a materialistic person, but this is her own way of expressing her lack of affection.*

*Marcela is weak because she is in conflict with herself; her vital energy is slipping away through the cracks generated by the two conflicting ideas. It is interesting to notice that every time she gives a step forward, something goes wrong. This is a confirmation that she is not "prepared," so she freezes. In her sense of self-compassion –one of the forms of anger that she is experiencing– she feels pity for herself, and this pity hurts her... So, she blames herself –another form of anger – and blame always asks to be punished. She does not take care of herself, has no regard for money and she exposes herself to relationships that have no future in sight... All of this in her desperate search for appreciation and gratefulness. However, they both escape her grasp because she can only find them where she has not looked for them: inside herself. This is her self-programming conflict.*

*It is worth taking some time to say a couple of things about Marcela's dog; the only being by whom she feels loved. Dogs are a model of fidelity to us humans (just as cats are a model of independence), something that is vital to the patient. However, even though she receives her dog's messages via telepathy, she looks for ways to deceive her because what she needs to learn from her canine friend is the lesson of being loyal to her own self...*

*"Find the meaning of your life and make it your goal."*

Carl Jung

## Marcela's Action Protocol:

1. *Elaborate on the grief and sorrow from having felt as an orphan (1), from your failed life's project, which ended with the abortion (2), and from the death of your partner in life (3).*
2. *Open yourself to the reality that every soul has a free will, and if your lover left, he must have had his own reasons. Recognize that with his death you have idealized him, and now you need to take him down from the altar in which you placed him.*
3. *Recognize that to feel guilty is a useless and contaminating feeling; stop feeling guilty!*
4. *Make the decision not to respond to other people's expectations, even if that "other" person is called "mother."*
5. *Honor your body and respect your limits.*
6. *Be more flexible with yourself, this will make it easier to respond to your needs. Allow*

pg. 113

*yourself to get help, orientation, or whatever you need.*

7. *Give yourself the right to use your hands only for what you wish to do, without fear of not performing well or making a mistake.*
8. *Accept that you deserve to have a fun job that does not require a lot of effort.*
9. *Give and receive with love, not with fear, guilt or expectations.*
10. *Become conscious of your inner strength. Decide your path and go toward what you really desire.*

# X

## "To see her makes me sick!"
*The story of Caridad, 72 years old*

Every time I go to my country I feel really bad. Not because of the things that happen there, but because of my mother... It gives me anxiety, insomnia and panic attacks. I get sick just to think about the trip! But at the same time, I have my daughter, grandchildren and a great-grandson over there. I go because of her and her children, which are my family.

I feel obligation toward my mother. Before I used to see her as someone large, imposing... now she is just a little thing. I can't leave her to her own fate! I would much rather giving her money or the things she needs, in exchange for her relieving me of the agony... To think that I am going to see her makes me sick... it gives me the creeps!

My daughter has problems. She feels bad very often, and then she wants to commit suicide. I have to give everything to her, poor child, because otherwise she has a real bad time. My son doesn't give me much trouble these days, but he also had it rough at one point in time. His wife cheated on him and it seems the other man didn't stick it out of her, so she tried to commit suicide. He took her back because their kids were suffering greatly. I continue to speak to her because my son loves her and she is a good mother; go figure, she's not bad with her kids.

Ever since I can remember, I have a feeling of being empty, not satisfied. I think one should feel full, satisfied. I don't have a solution for this.

All my life I lived waiting for the moment to ask one question to my mother. This question always seemed to be in the verge of strangling me... Why did you and dad leave me in another town when you guys got divorced? I finally gathered the strength to ask her when she was, supposedly, on her death bed. Her answer was: "Because your father was cheap and I was too young." I mean, woman, what kind of answer is that? I didn't want to justify her, but I decided to accept it. Why would I want to torment her? In the end, I already knew the answer. Of course she didn't die in that occasion, and I suspect that isn't going to happen any time soon... She's still going to take a few more to the tomb! However, I feel sorry that I don't seem to have any kind of feelings for her; the kind of feelings that I hope my children would feel for me...

My mom cheated on my father, and poor him living in a small town, his life became hell. He was so devastated that he couldn't take care of me, or who knows, maybe my mother protected me from raised by the mock of the town...

Still, I can't seem to understand how was it that I was not important to either one of my parents, to the degree that both were able to get rid of me as if I wasn't even born... How could my aunt love me more than them? Or, how could they continue with their lives and just assume that I was alright? I can't wrap my head around it!

Living with my aunt I didn't even have a bed, or anything of the sort. I lived with her since I was eight years old until I turned sixteen, when I got married. She raised me with lots of love; I can't complain about it. Despite the fact that she was so poor, she gave me the best she could... She was an old maid, go figure!

My aunt used to tell me: "You have to get married; otherwise you'll end up screwing up with some boy," or "Find a boyfriend and get married, before you end up screwing things up." Poor woman; she was obsessed with it, and in the end I got married to someone who made my life impossible!

My husband was very jealous… One night while I was asleep, he threatened me with a knife. He stabbed it in the night stand next to me and I woke up screaming. On another occasion, he wrapped himself up with some felt like material and poured alcohol all over him… he said he was going to start himself on fire! I got so afraid that I passed out. Finally I escaped with my kids to another province… and to have a hard time; my whole life was one of martyrdom!

After the bitterness I feel from having to go to my country, I also have to feel another kind… the bills I have to pay. Every time that I go there I get into debts, and then I cannot find the resources to pay for my credit cards. Over there they have no idea of everything that I go through in order to provide them with their needs, given that I live on retirement funds. Once I am back here, I feel as if I am going to have a panic attack because I don't have the resources to pay the bills; that's the worst thing that can happen to me!

## Caridad's Case Analysis

*Caridad arrives to the clinic with what appears to be a specific type of phobia. However, very soon we realize that she is really somaticizing her resentment towards her mother.*

*Symbolically speaking, the mother represents the heart of the home. Caridad's mother leaves with another man, which is not something usual in those times, though not something unheard of. What is unusual is the fact that she does it at the expense of leaving her daughter behind. With this action, Caridad's mother leaves some clear signs of certain issues that are difficult to deal with for Caridad, but that nonetheless are a source of internal torment for her. Such things are the following:*

1. *The mother is not woman enough to take her child with her, or she is openly rejecting her as the offspring of a very unsatisfactory relationship; the child of a man who did not perform to the standard.*
2. *The father is exposed as a failed "macho" who is not man enough to retain her woman, or take care of his own child...*

*Caridad has lost all family references. She feels that her own parents have given her the five wounds of her childhood: rejection, abandonment, betrayal, humiliation and injustice... Therefore, her inner child ends up feeling devalued in front of her parents, in front of everybody else, and as such, that is how she feels in her inner most self...*

*As a result of this, Caridad has a double sense of lack. On the one hand, she lacks affection (maternal role), on the other hand, she has economic deprivation (paternal role), because in a symbolic sense she is an orphan. She feels she does not deserve anything good in life because she has been disinherited. An inheritance is the result of legitimacy, and the consultant feels like she was more of a foster child. Her generalized state of anxiety comes from the fear of being punished, because she secretly desires to be compensated for her pain, as much as she desires to get revenge. The guilt she feels as a result of this makes her show herself as a compassionate and worthy person; she thinks this would redeem the clan, but given that this behavior is just a façade, all the effort she makes in pretending leaves her drained of her vital energy, and blocks her creativity to make money.*

*No matter how much love she received from her aunt, Caridad's life is barred, marked with a 'before' and an 'after.' That is why the consultant seems to be incapable of living in the present* moment. *She speaks a lot about her past, about what she went through and what happened to her; but she also worries incessantly about what could happen in the future...*

*She falls prey to some irrational beliefs that make her sink into hopelessness, and because of that, she has grown up in a state of perplexity that corrodes her from within. When she finally dares to speak about it, she did not get the response that would have helped to heal her inner child.*

*And so it is that, no matter at what cost, she goes to the rescue of her own daughter as a compulsion to prove that she is a "good mother", unlike hers. She thinks of herself as being someone essential to the lives of her children, without even realizing that they have not being doing well in life either, despite being provided with all of what she perceives she lacked.*

*As she feels that her mother did not give her anything, she feels that she means "nothing" to her. She thinks that she would only "torment" her if she were to communicate how she truly feels.*

*Her daughter's attempted suicide is both the result of a generational transmission, and that of Caridad's categorical "no" to a situation that she insists on denying. As a result, the inner bitterness that she feels toward love keeps growing. The basic belief is that to love means to suffer. It is interesting to note that her son attracts a woman that is both unfaithful and a potential suicide...*

*Caridad expresses a tone of docility, but in fact she lives with much internal anger, and she deeply rejects that feeling. Because of this, she lives an incoherent life; she punishes herself for the feeling by being hard on herself, and she denies herself the right to stop or do what she really likes. This appears in her speech as an inability to ask for what she needs. Her magical thought is that others are mind readers and that they will give her what she needs. Give that those people do not respond to her expectations, she feels disappointed and harbors more bitterness and rancor. She could even harbor a desire for revenge, even when she feels powerless. The whole situation makes her experience an anger that she properly suppresses, until she begins to somaticize...*

*She wants to receive, in fact, she is waiting for affection, she is thirsty for it; but she will never have enough until she stops giving and starts to ask. She is stuck in the culture that says that it is best to give, than it is to receive... this is Caridad's motto... and so her life reflects it. So many imbalances are created as a result of always taking for herself, or always giving to others, without opening or allowing herself to receive; if we don't balance this function (which is only one), life will turn us into beggars...*

pg. 122

*"There are so many depressed people in the world because the game of life is not as fun as they expected."*

Ram Dass

## Caridad's Action Protocol:

1. *As soon as you feel the onset of an anxiety attack, become conscious that it is your imagination taking control and confront it!*
2. *Recognize that it is not the circumstances of your life, but your emotions which paralyze you. Stop accumulating them!*
3. *Search yourself to find out why it is so hard for you to ask for what you need. Once you confront your truth... Ask!*
4. *Accept the idea that you can allow yourself to say "no" whenever you don't wish to do something, and if you decide to do it, do it with pleasure and without subjecting yourself to a useless inquisition.*
5. *If you are looking for recognition through your actions, confess it! There is nothing wrong about wanting to feel recognized when we do something for someone else. Whatever you choose to do, do it with joy; life will*

pg. 123

> *seems more pleasant and you will flow with the abundance of life.*

6. *Read about the stage of Integrity vs. Despair described by Erik Erikson. Complete your own vital cycle and leave a worthy legacy to the generations that will succeed you.*

7. *Enjoy your present, it is a gift.*

# Request from a child to its parents:

1.  Do not blame me for the circumstances of my conception, or the choice of couple that you made, or the quality of your life after my birth; I AM a blessing, not a disgrace or a shame.
2.  Always try to be a source of pride for me; remember that you are my main example in life.
3.  Never ask me which one I love more, mother or father, or tell me that I am yours, because that would exclude a half of me. Allow me to live in integrity.
4.  Never compare me with someone else; instead, emphasize and encourage my uniqueness. Above all, do not compare me with my progenitor in a negative way. It will be better if you tell me how beautiful, intelligent and good I AM, without conditions... the best vision that you can hold is the only blessing that I need to succeed in all aspects of my life.
5.  Do not project in me your unfulfilled dreams and wishes. I came with my own life's project, which will only be truncated if somehow you attempt to manipulate me into fulfilling yours.
6.  Invest some time, quality care and unconditional love in me when I need it, and

you will see me flourish as a functional, independent and happy being. In this way, you will avoid having to carry me on your back through life, or see me suffering the unspeakable…

7. Do not give me nicknames, make a ridicule of me or laugh at me. If you say ugly things to me, I will learn to accept that other do so as well; first, it will be my parents, then my peers and couples.

8. Do not criticize me, yell at me, insult or punish me… just tell me clearly what you expect from me and gently make me do the correct action.

9. Never tell me such things as: "who do you think you are?" If you do, I will convince myself that I am no body. Then, when you wanted me to be someone, I will not be able, because all my life I will have attempted to obey you.

10. Teach me useful things like discipline and organization, how to manage money and be a better communicator; to be proactive and how to choose a couple. Then, trust me to be able to put into practice what I have learned.

11. Show me, by example, how to eat right, exercise, and to care and respect my body.

12. If I tell you that I do not like hand plays or that I do not like to be tickled, respect my refusal. Only then will I be able to make my

refusal noteworthy if a situation arises in another context.

13. Don't talk to me about "dangers," instead, talk to me about goals; this way I will clearly know what to focus on.

14. Tell me the truth how and when it is appropriate; do not disturb me with your disharmonies, but please do not lie to me. For me, it is important to know the reason why things are the way they are, when they concern me. If you speak to me from your heart, I can understand everything, even from my level of understanding.

15. Keep your private life to yourself, whether it is good or bad. Do not share it with me. The details of your sexual life are none of my concern.

16. Allow me to say what I think because that which I do not express tortures my mind and sickens my body.

17. Allow me to express my emotional states, even if they are in disharmony, and validate them when I am right or help me to normalize them when I am over reacting. In this way, I will feel supported and learn to manage my emotions.

18. Beware of stalkers; especially if they are adults, whether they are family or not, close to the family, neighbors or teachers. The harassment of a couple, if it can be compared,

can be overcome with less difficulty than that of an authority figure.

19. Let me have power in my relationship with you; children that have power in their relationship with their parents grow up to assert their rights, and I need to practice in order to learn how to assert mines.

20. Give me the freedom to learn core responsibilities.

21. Allow me to experiment with the consequences of my actions. If you pretend to "save" me, you will only sentence me.

22. Do not pretend that I do not have to go through the same things you went through; that is your trauma speaking. Raise me with love, not fear.

23. Give me enough to do something, but no so much that I will not do anything else.

24. Encourage my creativity, not my obedience. If you kill my creativity, I will be less than what I can become. If you teach me blind obedience, I will listen to any voice that it is not my inner voice.

25. Do not rob me of my experience of life; when my time comes, I will be ready to fly. Look at me with admiration and let me go. Then, congratulate yourself... You did your work!

## Requests from a child to its separated or divorced parents:

1. Parents, if you are to separate in order to be happier, do it in harmony but without abandoning me; continue to care for and loving me in a way that I can feel it.
2. Separate or divorce if you are sure that it is the best for everyone involved, but do it with just as much or even more love than the one that brought you two together. If you do it that way, I will understand everything that you explain to me.
3. Avoid making a devil out of each other, just so that I do not ever have to listen to you insulting one another, or observe any kind of aggressive or passive-aggressive attitudes. That would only create a loyalty conflict within me.
4. Remember that I have two parents and I always want to have you both. I do not want to be afraid of showing you my love; allow me to love you both equally.
5. Mother/father: Never speak ill of my other parent; always remember that you chose her/him. There is no way to hate him/her without hating me, because you both are a part of me...
6. Do not use me as a weapon to throw at the other ("now you have to take him/her"); I would feel like you get rid of me at your convenience.

7. Do not kidnap me ("now you won't see him/her"); become knowledgeable about the parental alienation syndrome and do not abuse me. If I can share in a healthy way with both my mother and father, I will grow up integrating my feminine and masculine archetypes.
8. Do not interrogate me about the new house, the new couple or the new family; all that matters is whether I am well or not... I am not a spy.
9. Do not me get me into your bed because you need company, only to get me out of it as soon as you get someone; I am not a piece of furniture.
10. Do not tell me that now I am the "man of the house" or the "woman of the house." It was not my decision to live in a single parent home; allow me to live through each stage of my development.
11. Remember that a relationship never ends in the children they have together; in a child, there is 50% of the father and 50% of the mother cohabitating at all times. Respect yourselves so that you may be reconciled within me. If you really love me and wish to see me as a functional and happy being, then respect yourselves, whether it is face to face or in the distance, or even behind curtains...
12. Honor me, I AM a gift from life that gives you the opportunity to give the best of you and, in its appropriate time, receive the best of me with open arms and a humble heart.

## Positive affirmations for the inner child:

1. Even though my parents did not love me as I would have liked them to, I recognize that they have loved me in the best way they knew and could.
2. Even though my parents didn't take care of me in the way that I now judge they should have, or even if they didn't give what I now believe they should have given me, today, I stop judging them and holding irrational beliefs about them. Just to imagine the something worse could have happened, I realize that they did enough and gave me enough.
3. Even though my parents did not give me the recognition that I hoped for, today, I choose to recognize my multiple merits and accept myself as a valuable human being.
4. Today I recognize that if I do not love myself I cannot love anyone else, and because of that, I give up victimization, and choose to love me so that I can love others and live a plentiful life.
5. I do not try to do the opposite of what my parents did to me; that would mean that I continue to act based on my pain. Today, I

heal any resentment against my parents, and from my place of freedom, I choose to be the best parent that I can based in my love of self and the specific needs of my child (or each one of my children).

6. Today, I understand that my parents were not what I hoped for, but I did need them.

7. Today, I recognize that my parents are my mirror; I do not have the right to judge them, and I choose to honor them because they have shown me the aspect of myself that I deny.

8. Today, I accept my responsibility for having chosen my parents as the best teachers for what I needed to learn.

9. Today, I ask forgiveness and I forgive myself for the expectations that I had with respect to my parents, and I am capable of accepting them fully, with their virtues and defects.

10. Today, I ponder about their unfulfilled dreams to care for me and provide me, and I thank them for having given me life and the opportunity to make my own life.

11. Today, I take in their strength and move forward; now I am capable of letting love flow!

## ALEXANDRA MAS

Studied Humanities, Drama, Modern Languages and Translation at the University of Puerto Rico, her birth country.

At Isla del Encanto, she worked as an actress, model, entertainment critic, news reporter and TV and radio host for several relevant shows. She also appeared in theater, soap operas, TV commercials, publicity voice over and the "Artistas" magazine's opinion column.

In Madrid, Spain, Alexandra expanded her educational background with a masters degree in film acting. She also worked in short-films, voice acting, and she also appeared on a TV show that reported on various subjects.

In 1994 she moved to the United Stated with her two sons.

Once in Miami, Florida, she obtained an M.S. in Psychology Major in Marriage and Family Therapy, at the Carlos Albizu University.

Later on, she studied hypnotherapy at the Santiago Aranegui School of Mystical and Philosophical Arts. Nowadays, she holds annual psychology courses for hypnotherapists.

Due to her long experience as a communicator, and her lengthy studies as a Psychologist, she is a customary guest at various radio and TV shows, where she is invited in order to give her expert opinion regarding various subjects in psychology.

(http://www.youtube.com/=Alexandra+Mas+habla)

Currently, Alexandra Mas hosts the radio show "Querer es poder," for personal growth and motivation. The show is broadcasted every day at 3:00pm, with a rebroadcast at 8:00pm (East time), via 153 Sirius XM (http://www.siriusxm.com.) She also collaborates with "OM Times Magazine."

(http.//editions.omtimes.com/magazine)

Mrs. Alexandra Mas uses the various techniques of Systemic Therapy, Psychogenealogy and Bioneuroemotion – amongst others – very effectively. A Motivator by excellence, she is dedicated to transforming the lives of others from her consultation room, via Skype, radio shows, and through her various talks, courses and seminars, amongst which it is important to highlight "Constelaciones Familiares."

Currently, she is happily married.

To check her motivational "tweets", follow Alexandra Mas on:
Twitter@Alexandra Mas
Facebook/Alexandra Mas
www.masporlafamilia.com

# GLOSSARY

**Abuse Cycle** = The classic abusive relationship is characterized by a three-stage cycle that may or may not be visible to outsiders. *The Tension-Building Stage* is the phase of insidious and progressive control in which the abuser becomes increasingly remote, contemptuous, critical, preoccupied, or otherwise on edge. *The Abuse Stage* follows when the abuser actively looks for excuses to blow up over, by setting his/her partner up in a *no-win situation. The Remorse Stage:* Occurs when having blown off steam and regaining composure, the abusive person is full of apologies and promises never to do "it" again. The abuser can be so charming and complimentary that the codependent victim's heart breaks. The more codependent and insecure the partner, the more vulnerable they are to the partner's *attentive remorse.* Abusers during this phase behave like a "normal" person but their fear inevitably powers the resumption of the abuse cycle.

**Alpha Male** = In social animals, it is the individual with the highest rank in the community, to whom the others follow. In humans, this expression refers to a man in a high position, similar to the hegemonic masculinity. A son may desire to become the alpha male in his family, just as a separated or divorced women may ask a male son to assume the role of the "man of the house."

**Archetype** = Original pattern or model from which other objects, ideas or concepts are derived. According to Plato, archetypes are the substantial forms of those things that exist eternally. According to Carl Gustav Jung, archetypes are autonomous ancestral images which are the basic constituents of Humanity's Collective Unconscious.

**Aspect** = According to the Emotional Freedom Technique (EFT, also known as "Tapping"), certain issues cannot completely be resolved because they are composed of many aspects or parts. It could be thoughts, beliefs, impressions or emotions, etc, which, when it comes to the unconscious mind, are separate subjects. A patient cannot usually make such distinction, but once there is some improvement, the facilitator has to detect them all, in order to work with each one separately.

**Attachment** (Figure of) = A person with whom one seeks to establish a relationship with the most immediate goal of pursuing and sustaining a proximity in times of threat, as it provides safety, comfort and protection. The term comes from *John Bowlby's Attachment Theory*. He describes two patterns: *Secure Attachment* and *Anxious-resistant Insecure Attachment* (also called ambivalent attachment). The *Anxious-Ambivalent/Resistant strategy* is a response to unpredictably responsive caregiving, and the displays of anger or helplessness towards the caregiver on reunion can be regarded as a conditional strategy for maintaining the availability of the caregiver by preemptively taking control of the interaction.

**Bioneuroemotion** = An approach to healing developed by Enric Corbera and his team, based on *New German Medicine, Biological Decoding,*

*Psychogenealogy, Psychogenetic System, Cellular Memory, Psychosomatics, Total Biology* and other approaches, along with the guidelines of *A Course in Miracles*. Its premise is that sickness is a biological program of survival and adaptation to an event that is so shocking that it is suppressed and, since its resolution is left unfinished, it becomes fixed in time, thus, somatized. Once the conflict or bioshock is revealed, it is treated with a mix of *Ericksonian Hypnosis*, *NLP*, or *Sophrology* techniques, as the main intervention therapies. This accomplishes the release of the Bioneuroemotion that causes many physical illnesses.

**Clan** = Concept that goes back to the origins of the human race, when there were small communities where everybody lived together and acted in the same way, caring for the wellbeing of the group and without individual desire, given that everyone's survival (the individual's and the group's) depended on not getting out of the group.

**Conflict** = The remnants of how a certain experience has affected a person. According to Bioneuroemotion, behind the physical symptoms there are always one or more conflicts. There are many types of it, and they can be divided into two main categories: Programming and trigger. There is a need to clarify that there are situations that are so shocking in the life of a person, that they can turn into both programming and trigger conflicts at the same time.

1) **Programming Conflict** –Emotional impact caused by an event external to the individual and which records certain information in the unconscious mind, probably without causing any symptoms. This is usually lived between conception

and adolescence, a stage in which the mind and the biology of the person are very receptive, and are particularly working at the same time. The self-programming conflict has no need for an external event; the person is self-programmed by his/her beliefs and way of seeing the world, in a manner that creates a conflict for the self that later on feeds off itself.

2) **Trigger conflict** –Emotional impact that is related to the programming conflict with regards to the emotional tone, and when it shows up, it opens and activates the previous conflict, triggering a symptom or disease as a biological reaction of survival. The treatment needs to start here, but the programming conflict has to be deactivated in order for the symptom or disease to subside.

**Childhood Decision** = Decision made by a child, not having the maturity to make such decision yet. For example: "When I grow up, I will smoke like my father does" or "When I grow up, I won't be like my mom." A very common one amongst sterile women is the following: "I won't have kids so they won't go through all I went through," etc.

**Childhood Wound** = According to Lise Bourbeau, *Rejection, Abandonment, Humiliation, Betrayal* and *Injustice* are the five wounds that prevent a person from being truly itself.

- An adult with the *Rejection Wound* will have the tendency to reject itself and others, as well as pleasant experiences and success. The person will become the "elusive" one because of the wrong belief of not being worthy.

- An adult with the *Abandonment Wound* will have the tendency to abandon projects and partners. This person will become dependent until becoming aware of its lack of unconditional love and becomes responsible for its own life, so it is able to overcome this sense of loneliness.

- An adult with the *Humiliation Wound* tends to be insecure, shy and hesitant, and in the depths of its being, the person feels guilty and believes it has no right to basic rights; it can even doubt its own right to exist.

- An adult with the *Betrayal Wound* does not allow itself to trust anything or anyone. Its worst fear is a lie, so this person will become a controller. Most of the people that exhibit extreme jealousy have had experiences of betrayal in their childhood.

- An adult with the *Injustice Wound* will behave rigidly; will tend to look for perfection because of its great fear is making a mistake, which brings much frustration. Its great challenge is to become flexible and humble in order to heal.

One has to work on healing these wounds in order to stop repeating dysfunctional behavioral patterns and to avoid a blind generational transmission of them.

**Comfort Zone** = A state within which a person feels that uncertainty, scarcity and vulnerability are minimized, where an individual believe will have access to enough love, food, talent, time, admiration, thus a sense of control. An environment in which such a person thinks it is easy to get more satisfaction and results with less effort or without risk.

**Delusional Focus** = Sense of injustice that becomes a person's *recurring central motif*; it is like the leitmotiv of a literary work or a film.

**Diagnosis Conflict** = Impression generated when a specialist communicates the patient the diagnosis of a condition, particularly if it is considered chronic, if it is lived as a *biological shock*. In this kind of trance, the individual *introjects* the beliefs of that authority figure, along with associated personal meanings. The person ends up trapped in a belief or set of beliefs that is not his/hers.

**Differentiation** = A person's ability to separate his/her intellectual and emotional functioning from those of the person's family of origin. The term was coined by Murray Bowen, who had a scale to measure a person's progress from *poorly differentiated*, to *well differentiated*.

**Double Bind** = Described by Gregory Bateson as an emotionally distressing dilemma in communication in which an individual receives two or more conflicting messages, and one message negates the other. This creates a situation in which a successful response to one message results in a failed response to the other (and vice versa), so that the person will automatically be wrong regardless of response. The double bind occurs when the person cannot confront the inherent dilemma, and therefore can neither resolve it nor opt out of the situation. Double binds are often utilized as a form of control without open coercion—the use of confusion makes them both difficult to respond to as well as to resist.

**Emergent** = Term coined by philosopher G. H. Lewes to refer to the new, resulting product from a previous situation. In families or other groups, it refers to the most advanced individual; the one who resist or call for a change.

**Emotional Orphan** = An individual who had suffered abuse and abandonment and who had learned in consequence that trust in others is their most bitter enemy.

**Factor of Attraction** = The predominant thought processes of a person at any given moment. This establishes an emotion, a belief system and as such, a life experience. If the life experience is unsatisfactory, one has to become aware of his/her factor of attraction and change it.

**Fallen "Macho"** = A man who does not exercise what is considered to be the masculine role in a given society. This kind of man has usually been "castrated" by his mother, and if he manages to differentiate from their family of origin, he will attract a "woman with a phallus" (a woman that holds a masculine role in that society).

**Family Constellations** = A therapeutic method developed by Bert Hellinger which draws on elements of *Family Systems Therapy*, *Existential Phenomenology* and Zulu attitudes to family, and incorporates the idea of *morphic resonance* into his explanation of it. The rationale is that present-day problems and difficulties may be influenced by traumas suffered in previous generations of the family, even if those affected now are unaware of the original event in the past. So, in a single session it attempts to reveal a previously unrecognized *systemic dynamic* that spans multiple generations to resolve the deleterious effects of it by encouraging the subject to accept the factual reality of the past.

**Grieving Process** = The course of the process from the moment a loss occurs until it is overcome. It is the experience of emotional adjustment that follows any loss (the death of a loved one, the end of a relationship or a job, the loss of the country by the process of emigration, etc.) This elaboration includes the emotional response to the loss in its spiritual, mental, emotional, physical, behavioral, and social dimensions.

**Identified Patient** = Clinical term that refers to a person to which the family or other system (group) assigns the cause of a problem, or the one that is said to suffer from a pathology. From the point of view of the *systemic approach*, the therapeutic action will focus not only on that single individual, but mainly on the relationships and interactions of the *family system*.

**Identity Crisis** = According to psychologist Erik Erikson, it is the failure to achieve ego identity during adolescence. The stage of psychosocial development in which identity crisis may occur is called the *Identity Cohesion* versus *Role Confusion* stage. During adolescence, teenagers face physical growth, sexual maturation, and have to integrate ideas of themselves with what others think of them. Adolescents therefore form their self-image and endure the task of resolving the crisis of their basic ego identity. Successful resolution of the crisis depends on one's progress through previous developmental stages, centering on issues such as trust, autonomy, and initiative.

**Imago** = The unconscious image of the opposite sex that we carry within us and that we have *introjected* from our parents, which is what we'll end up attracting as a partner. The *Imago Therapy* seeks to ensure that the members of a couple become conscious of these models, which are mistaken in many occasions, in order to be free from those *mental constructs* and accept their partner's essential being.

**Individuation** = The way in which an individual is identified as distinguished from other individuals. The overarching goal of *Jungian Analytical Psychology* is the attainment of self through individuation.

**Induct** = An induced belief, almost always by repetition, which functions as an *unconscious mandate* (like a hypnotic suggestion).

**Informed Patient** = A patient that has gone through several therapeutic processes (typically without finishing them) thus is familiar with clinical terminology and applies to him/herself. If the patient did not use all of that information "against" him/herself, it would be easier to help.

**Insecure Attachment** = John Bowlby's *Attachment Theory* establishes that the kids that grow up with parents or caretakers (*attachment figures*) who display an inconsistent pattern of availability or shows of affection, will later on display a pattern of relationships dominated by distrust, because this *attachment modality* will have adversely interfered with their exploratory capacity.

**Introjection** = Messages from our figures of authority which govern our life from the unconscious level. Since they are inductions of fear, we tend to obey them blindly. When they are identified, we can easily get rid of them because they are just acquired *irrational beliefs*.

**Invisible Children** = Children who suffer from the indifference of their parents and adults who are emotionally significant to them. Being ignored cause undesirable consequences that contaminate all areas of these children's lives. To solve these problems, psychologist Martha Alicia Chavez recommends to carry out a process of inner healing, to allow for the recognition of others, internalize be seen and thus quench the thirst of it.

**Irrational Beliefs** = Ideas, feelings, beliefs, ways of thinking, attitudes, opinions, biases, prejudices, or values with which we were raised. We have become accustomed to using them when faced with problems in our current life, even when they are not productive in helping us reach a positive, growth-enhancing solution.

**Life Proiect** = A mission to live well and give well bv becoming a creator, a leader, a mentor, a giver, a doer.

**Love Movement Interrupted** = When the child has been removed too early from the mother, father or both, it is said that there has being a love movement interrupted. This child will lose confidence in the mother, father or both, for fear of having to suffer the pain of that loss once again, even if the parents take care of the child in a loving way after the separation. The child will attempt not to disappoint others as he/she was disappointed, will suffer from trust issues in his/her adult life and ultimately will procure to exclude him/herself as a defense mechanism.

**Magical Thinking** = Thought process based on religious faith, imagination, desires, emotions, traditions or even superstitions, which generates cognitions devoid of fundamental logic. The correlation is often between religious ritual, prayer, sacrifice or the observance of a taboo, and an expected benefit or on the contrary experience fear of performing certain acts or having certain thoughts because of an assumed correlation between doing so and threatening calamities.

**Mirror** = A person that reflects back to us characteristics that we would like to consciously hide, but that we unconsciously are... or judge. In the mirror (the other person), we project the aspects of ourselves that we deny, at the same time that our unconscious generates the illusion of separation. We are born in the midst of relationships and throughout our lives we seek to relate to others in different contexts, because love is a magnetic force; an energy of union. The mirror exists as a tool to ensure gaining awareness of the primordial truth we are all one.

**Mirror Work** = An exercise proposed by Louise Hay that consist in looking at oneself in a mirror, thoroughly and systematically (face first and then the naked body). The idea is to allow the hidden emotions to surface, as well as their inner dialogues, in order to identify any programming and expose false identities. When the mind is silent and the person is devoid of emotion, the goal is to reprogram the mind with *Positive Affirmations*.

**Neuro-linguistic Programming (NLP)** = Model of interpersonal communication that deals with the relationship between successful behavior, subjective experiences and, in particular, the thought process. As a therapeutic system, it aims at educating people in self-awareness and effective communication, in order to replace inefficient mental and emotional models of conduct, by effective ones that will allow the client to achieve his/her life goals.

**No-win Situation** = Also called a "lose-lose situation". it is a circumstance where a person has choices. but no choice leads to a net gain. See *Double Bind*.

**Other** = Psvchoanalvtic term that represents another person (the other) as well as the "otherness" as the conception of the external. Thus, the *Other*, or Another, is any person in relation to the *Self.*

**Parental Alienation** = Occurs when parents with children senarate or divorce. and one narent (usuallv the custodial narent) nurnoselv alienates the child or children from the non-custodial narent. The *Alienatino Parent* attemnts to damae or sever the child's relationship with the non-custodial parent.

**Parentification** = The process of role reversal whereby a child is obliged to act as parent to his/her own parent. In extreme cases, the child is used to fill the void of the alienating parent's emotional life. Two modes have been identified: *Instrumental Parentification* (involves the child completing physical tasks for the family, such as looking after a sick relative, paying bills, or providing assistance to younger siblings that would normally be provided by a parent) and *Emotional Parentification* (when a child or adolescent must take on the role of a confidant or mediator for, or between parents and/or family members).

**Parental Child** = A child that fulfills the role of one of the parents; a role that does not belong to him/her. The child can turn into a "hero" or "rescuer," but will always looking for gratitude and appreciation. When that child becomes an adult, there is an open or covert resentment for not having had the usual experiences of childhood and/or adolescence. Some deny themselves the experience of parenthood or do not take care of their own children as they could, because they performed that role earlier in their lives or because they continue to perform that role for their adult co-dependent siblings.

**Part** = See **Sub-personalities**

**Passive Death Wish** = Recurring thought of annihilation that can be verbalized or just thought of, but it is always felt. The person would not commit suicide, but would gladly die because he/she cannot see the end to the situation that is oppressing him/her. The person thinks such things as: "I would like to go to sleep and never wake up" or "If I die, all my problems would be over once and for all." This is one of the classic symptoms of depression.

**Patient's Speech** = Psychoanalytic term referred to the story that brings the client to the clinic, and which constitutes the material for analysis. It is the explanation that we give to our problems which, if it were true, we would not have any kind of problems. The issue is that we search for explanations (excuses, rationalizations, etc) in the conscious mind, when the real cause to our challenges lies in our *Unconscious Programming* running in automatic.

**Pathological Grief** = The reluctance to experience grief, because of attitudes about grieving and personality variables which predispose some people to difficult grieving. Sufferers may avoid sharing grief with the family physician, who may then fail to recognize it. There are four types of pathological grief: *chronic, inhibited, delayed,* and *atypical.* Failure to grieve may also lead to a higher incidence of physical disease and various forms of mental illness. In order to manage grief, the individual must be encouraged to express sadness, anger, and guilt; be reassured that these feelings are a normal reaction to loss; and later, be given permission to stop grieving. Although the incidence of pathological grief does not appear to be high, the morbidity and mortality of sufferers is significant.

**Place without a place** = The "non-place" destined for the person that, is "invisible" in his/her family and its voice is not heard (not taken into consideration). It is often a non-desired child or the opposite sex expected.

**Primordial Wound** = Feeling of separation (some say of God, others of the mother), which is the root and origin of all our psychic and spiritual "evils." In some philosophies, it refers to the conscious awareness of death.

**Program** = Unconscious mandate with coded instructions for the automatic performance of a particular task. It is always fulfilled until one becomes aware of it. It is usually a *transgenerational transmission,* but it can also be acquired through culture. A *programmed person* is not free to make his/her own decisions, but instead these *invisible forces* govern his/her life. It is necessary to be free in order to walk one's own path of evolution in life. If an individual is able get rid of his/her unconscious programming, it is said that he/she has had a *noble incarnation.*

**Psychomagic Act** = According to the creator of *Psychomagic* (a therapeutic-artistic discipline),

Alejandro Jodorowsky, it is a magic-symbolic-sacred act that interlaces shamanism, psychoanalysis and the pathetic effect of theater. The premise is that the unconscious mind takes symbolic acts as if they were real events, so that one could modify the unconscious behavior, and as result, overcome certain psychological traumas. These acts must be designed according to the client, and they are prescribed after having performed a study of the client's individual characteristics and analyzed his/her family tree.

**Psychogenealogy** = Theory and therapeutic modality developed by Alejandro Jodorowsky, according to which events, secret traumas and conflicts lived by our ancestors, will condition the weaknesses that constitute an individual, as well as his/her psychological problems and illnesses, and will account for any strange and inexplicable behaviors of the patient. This unconscious transmission prevents the subject from self-realization, so in order to become aware of them and be able to disassociate from them, it is necessary to study the patient's family tree.

**Recumbent Syndrome** = The *Recumbent Statue Syndrome*, as called by Dr. Salomon Sellam, describes a set of clinical, psychological and behavioral signs that present a person that is directly related to one (or many) death (s) which is (are) qualified as unjustifiable by the family (clan). In an unconscious process of *Transgenerational Repair* (due to pathological grief), a substitute child is programmed to represent and/or "make the deceased alive." For as long as this individual is unaware of what is going on, he/she will present a series of symptoms (behavioral, organic or psychic) in connection with the inability to live his/her own life. The key phrase is: "I feel that I am not living my own life." This syndrome already is part of

*Psychogenealogy,* *Psychosomatic* and *Bioneuroemotion* nomenclature; therapeutic modalities that deal with diminishing its effects.

**Reframing** = A technique from Aaron Beck's *Cognitive Therapy*. To reframe is to actively search for alternate ways to see ideas, events, situations and people in a way that will take us away from the automatic way of thinking which causes us psychobiological damage.

**Repair** = In *Transgenerational Therapy*, the term refers to a Symbolic Restitution, which seeks to bring the patient back to harmony so that he/she can lead a fulfilling life.

**Resource** = Internal state necessary to move through a critical situation that has caused a *Negative Programming*. When this situation is revived in the present, today's adult will take notice of what his/her inner child (or adolescent) is missing, and (in a disassociated state) will deliver it, for example, power. A physiological reaction will be evidence of the acceptance of the resource. Now the client is ready to re-live the situation and program a positive feeling instead.

**Scapegoat** = The individual who takes on the load of the unconscious emotional issues of his/her family. Generally speaking, it is the more sensitive member to the *Family Shadow* (the secrets of the family and its accompanying sense of guilt). According to a *Systemic/Transgenerational* Psychotherapy approach, it is the most loyal member of a family that, through his/her own challenges ends up helping to maintain the family's cohesiveness. Usually is identified as "the black sheep."

**Secondary Gain** = Significant benefit (or set of benefits) earned on an illness or problem that do not exist when the person is healthy. The most immediate are attention and affection. Another possibility is the temporary suspension of the usual obligations.

**Shadow** = Reservoir of our denied and/or suppressed aspects, which become predominant in key moments of our lives so that we can see, and come to terms with it.

**Somatize** (to) = Term attributed to Wilhelm Stekel, one of Sigmund Freud's first disciples. It describes the unconscious process of converting a mental state (as depression or anxiety) into physical symptoms. Since our defense mechanisms forbid us to consciously express what concerns us, so then the mind channels it in the form of physical bodily complaints in the absence of a known medical condition.

**Soul of the Family** = According to Bert Hellinger's *Family Constellations*, it is the force that takes care of the sense of belonging and wellbeing of all members of a family so that each one can serve the group. In this way, the system is steered in a certain direction as a "clan". If the wellbeing of all concerned is not being procured, a guilt feeling surfaces in order to regulate and reorient the individual to the wellbeing of the clan.

**Specific Phobia** = Persistent and irrational fear of a particular object, animal, activity or situation which poses little or no real danger to the person. The most common are: blood, injections (and other medical procedures), certain animals (e.g., spiders, dogs or snakes), enclosed spaces, heights, lightning or flying.

**Sub-personalities** = Also known as *Parts*, which hold beliefs and extreme emotions as a result of terrible childhood traumas and betrayals that the person who is expressing them has suffered during his/her childhood.

**Symptomatic Member** = A member of a family identified as the one who "has problems." This individual is referred to as "prone to be ill," "unstable," with "bad luck" or even the one who "ruins the life" of others, but in reality he/she is the *bearer of the family dysfunction*.

**Systemic Therapy** = Psychotherapeutic approach that differs from Family Therapy in the sense that the family is not the focus of therapeutic care, but the dynamics of the communication processes, the interactions between the members of system and the *subsystems* that compose it. In this way, both its concepts as well as its therapeutic techniques can be applied to couple's relationships, work teams, school contexts and individuals.

**Tangential Father** = A father that, although present at home or in the life of his child, is *psychologically absent* and therefore remains *emotionally unavailable*.

**Transference** = Psychoanalytic term that refers to the unconscious redirection to a substitute, of old feelings, affections, expectations or suppressed desires and emotions that were originally felt in childhood. The object of the transference could be a therapist in a phase of analysis called *transference neurosis* or any other new relationship.

**Transgenerational** = The transmission of genetic and energetic information from one generation to the next. In this way, either a trait or a conflict can be equally passing across generations. This can only be transmitted on a voluntary basis, so that a soul using its free will chooses to bring a family tree conflict into resolution. Since our memory is erased at birth, if we fail to awaken to what has to be done, we will have to endure the consequences of this *blind transgenerational transmission*.

**Unfinished Business** = Term of *Gestalt Therapy*. that refer to the unexpressed feelings that are associated with distinct memories and fantasies. These feelings may be resentment. rage. hatred. pain. anxiety. grief. guilt. and abandonment that are not fully experienced in awareness. so they linger in the background. and are carried into the present causing preoccupations. compulsive behaviors. wariness. and other self-defeating behaviors. Unfinished business will persist until the person faces and deals with these denied or alienated feelings.

**Vibrational Affinity** = In the flow of thought, humans are close to each other due to their essences vibrational affinity.
Humanity is entirely related from a fractal network of all its streams of thought. These networks are *morphic fields*, which come to be human-scale adaptation of the so called "collective instinct" of animals. Within these morphogenetic fields, vibration form families in which its components are linked in their evolutionary path.

**Vilify** = From the Latin Vilis Facer, a term commonly used in *Systemic Therapy* and it is used to show contempt for a person with either words or actions.

# EPILOGUE

The collection of cases presented in this book is based on true stories, but certain circumstances and names have been changed in order to protect the identity of their protagonists. Any similarity between someone with any of the names used in this book and their own personal story is pure coincidence.

The commentaries at the end of each story are my subjective analysis of these cases; clinical at times, other times not. In either case, they do not represent the opinions of other professional in the field of Mental Health, or Psychology as a body of knowledge.

The protocols and/or suggestions do not constitute or substitute a therapeutic process. If the reader feels the need of psychological help (or know of someone that needs it), seek the assistance of a trained and licensed professional; someone to engage in a therapeutic relationship that will help you to achieve a significant progress.

If you decide to start a therapeutic process, do not waste time in sessions that do not provide results. A psychologist or a psychotherapist is an agent of change, and psychotherapy is not a social relationship; it is an evolutionary process.

# BIBLIOGRAPHY

Your body's telling you: Love yourself!,
Lise Bourbeau

*Biodescodificación: el código secreto del síntoma*,
Enric Corbera and Rafael Marañon

Invisible Children, Martha Alicia Chavez

On-line Universal Encyclopedia

www.ingramcontent.com/pod-product-compliance
Lightning Source LLC
LaVergne TN
LVHW011332080426
835513LV00006B/300